A LITTLE BIT
OF
AURAS

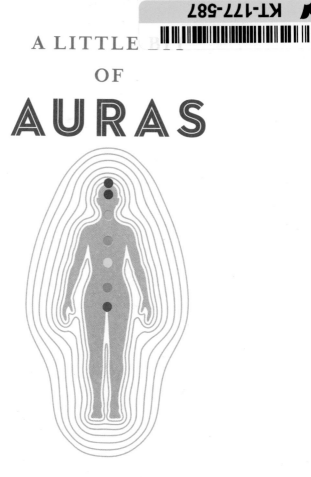

AN INTRODUCTION TO
ENERGY FIELDS

CASSANDRA EASON

STERLING ETHOS
New York

STERLING ETHOS

New York

An Imprint of Sterling Publishing
1166 Avenue of the Americas
New York, NY 10036

ISBN 978-1-4549-2853-9

Distributed in Canada by Sterling Publishing Co., Inc.
c/o Canadian Manda Group, 664 Annette Street
Toronto, Ontario, M6S 2C8, Canada
Distributed in the United Kingdom by GMC Distribution Services
Castle Place, 166 High Street, Lewes, East Sussex, BN7 1XU, England
Distributed in Australia by NewSouth Books
45 Beach Street, Coogee, NSW 2034, Australia

For information about custom editions, special sales, and premium and corporate purchases,
please contact Sterling Special Sales at 800-805-5489 or specialsales@sterlingpublishing.com.

Manufactured in China

2 4 6 8 10 9 7 5 3 1

sterlingpublishing.com

Interior design by Lorie Pagnozzi
Cover design by Elizabeth Mihaltse Lindy

Image Credits
Illustrations on page 4, 33, 51 , Britt Sabo
Shutterstock.com: DeoSum (body); satit_srihin (border);
solarus (background)

CONTENTS

INTRODUCTION...vii

❧ 1 ❧ THE COLORS OF THE AURA.............................. I

❧ 2 ❧ MORE AURA COLORS I5

❧ 3 ❧ EXPLORING THE MOOD AURA...........................27

❧ 4 ❧ UNDERSTANDING THE PERSONALITY AURA 39

❧ 5 ❧ CLEANSING, HEALING, AND ENERGIZING AURAS ...49

❧ 6 ❧ STRENGTHENING AND MAINTAINING
AURA HEALTH 6I

❧ 7 ❧ AURAS IN THE HOME AND WORKPLACE..............73

❧ 8 ❧ THE AURAS OF PETS 85

❧ 9 ❧ SEALING AND PROTECTING THE AURA
IN DAILY LIFE...97

ABOUT THE AUTHOR.....................................IO7

INDEX...IO8

INTRODUCTION

PICTURE THE GLOW SURROUNDING YOUNG LOVERS, OR A CHILD enchanted by a magical Santa grotto. The glittering grotto might be decorated with tinseled fairies. Saints, like those in traditional paintings, are portrayed with their heads surrounded by a golden sphere. People may say, if someone makes them angry, *I saw red* or *She was green with envy* because that is the main color being radiated and picked up intuitively without being physically seen. Auras like these are part of our natural perception of the world. In early societies, hunters looking out from a cave high in the hills would know if distant approaching tribesmen had friendly intentions by the energies they emitted.

We all have an aura, a rainbow-colored energy field, usually invisible to the physical eye, which can be perceived psychically with remarkably little practice. Our aura surrounds our whole body in a three-dimensional ellipse, made up of seven different-colored bands. This aura reveals our mood, our personality, and the status of our health. Our aura may guide our interactions with others, even though our actions may run counter to outward logical signs. Yet, invariably our aura-prompted actions are startlingly accurate.

At its most radiant and strong, the aura can reach outward to an extended arm span around the body. This spiritual bioenergetic aura field varies in size and density under different conditions. Gautama Buddha, the spiritual leader on whose teachings Buddhism was founded, was said to have an aura that extended over a range of several miles and therefore influenced people throughout that area.

In this book you will learn a variety of techniques for sensing, seeing, and interpreting your own aura and those of individuals and groups, as well as those of your pets. You will also discover how to cleanse, heal, strengthen, and protect the aura and how to use it both to create a good impression and to repel malice.

UNDERSTANDING THE AURA

Auras surround people, animals, plants, crystals, and even places. With practice, auras are easily sensed or seen clairvoyantly, using the innate psychic abilities we all possess. Through *claircognizance*, or the psychic sixth sense, we know intuitively the colors of an individual's aura. Using *psychometry*, or psychic touch, we can feel with the fingertips the health and colors of the aura. And with *clairvoyance*, we see the aura with the mind's eye. Some learn to see the aura externally.

The spiritual energy bands that make up the aura become progressively less dense and more ethereal the farther from the physical body they extend. The outermost levels—in blue, indigo, and violet—are the highest spiritually, until at the edges of the aura our aura energies merge as pure white light and gold with the cosmos. Sometimes one or more layers can predominate and seem to cover the whole aura. Or they may appear to be pale or missing altogether, depending on the current state of our health and what is happening in our lives. Though our aura has seven layers, a number of people operate mainly through the innermost four layers. Indeed, the more you work with the aura, the more in tune you become with your spiritual energies and your angels and spirit guides.

SOURCES OF AURA ENERGIES

Aura energy is transmitted to and from the body via seven main invisible energy centers, called chakras, as well as numerous other smaller or energy channels.

These energy centers are part of the inner spiritual or etheric body made of light, the part of us that survives death. The pure, white-light energies from our spiritual self are diffused or split into the seven strands of rainbow light that radiate beyond and around the whole body and are most clearly seen around the head and shoulders. In practice, the auras around the head and neck are the most accessible to cleansing, sealing against stress or unkindness, and healing. The effects of positive intervention can be experienced through the whole aura and the body and mind.

Each chakra is fueled by and empowers a specific aura layer of the same color, as noted in Chapter 5 (page 49). Your aura is empowered by individual energy fields of other people and your pets in the form of love, loyalty, acceptance, and approval.

Our energy fields are also depleted by noise; pollution; rays from computers, televisions, mobile phones, and electrical appliances; toxins; and by negative or controlling behavior of other people, such as unfair criticism, coldness, spite, or possessiveness. Aura protection is as vital at night as locking your front door, because sometimes free-floating or deliberate negativity can adversely affect your aura while you sleep, when it is most vulnerable.

THE UNIVERSAL ENERGY FIELD

The universal energy field, perceived as pure, white light—the colors of the rainbow synchronized together—flows into each individual aura and itself receives impressions and feelings from individual auras, again in constant interchange. It is the pure life force, called *qi* in the Japanese tradition, *chi* by the Chinese, *prana* in Hindu spirituality, *mana* in Hawaii, and in the Hebrew world *ruach*.

The life force can be absorbed into your aura through natural food, water, and fresh juices, and in any unprocessed food such as meat, fruit, grains, and vegetables.

The universal energy field is made up of the collective energies of other people, places, animals, and sources of the life force, such as crystals, flowers, the sun, the moon, astrological influences, and seasonal flows, so it is constantly changing. The wisdom of angels and spirit guides enters through our personal energy field. This personal energy field also encompasses the universal experiences and the wisdom of people in all times and places. Our personal aura contains the experiences of our past lives and the wisdom we have acquired from ancestors, recent and ancient.

In addition, collective energy fields accumulate over buildings, from homes and workplaces to abbeys and ancient sites, such as battlefields, and these collective energy fields remain associated with those sites. These are the energies released by the individuals who lived and worked or died there at different times. For this reason, you may sense a happy atmosphere in an ancient monastery where different generations lived quiet, contemplative, and unvarying existences over a period of centuries. By contrast, a battlefield will feel dark even centuries later because of all the suffering and brutality inflicted there, and these impressions are especially strong on the anniversary of the tragedy.

INTERPRETING THE AURA

Young children, who are naturally clairvoyant yet have never studied or heard of the concept of auras, routinely see and often draw colors around people and say, *Oh that is a green lady* or *a pink cat,* because they are picking up the essential feelings or character of the subject. As children acquire more education and learn that cats are physically black, white, and brown, but never pink, the physical vision of what is tangibly visible takes over. But the ability to detect and interpret auras never goes away.

SENSING THE AURA

Most aura awareness in everyday life comes through sensing the aura of others, and we all do this unconsciously. When someone you do not know or do not like gets too close, even if he is not physically touching you, you may feel uncomfortable because he is intruding on your aura or *personal space.* By contrast, when a small child or your lover snuggles up to you, there is no defining barrier between you and the other person; the energy field boundaries have relaxed and flowed temporarily into one.

FEELING YOUR RAINBOW

Even though aura colors may not be physically seen, the mood or a person's personality is being transmitted as one or more colors and experienced as a sensation. Some seriously visually impaired people, especially if they once had good vision, can distinguish between colors by touch. Those who are color-blind also rapidly learn through touch the different energies and strengths of the aura and can feel, for example, the power of red and discriminate the different shades, whether passionate or furious. So, too, in healing can knots and tangles be felt.

Red feels hot and strong; orange feels warm and confident; yellow feels focused and stimulates ideas; green feels gentle and flowing; blue feels cool, calm, and rippling; indigo feels peaceful and uplifting; and violet brings spiritual insights and maybe sudden awareness of the presence of an angel or spirit guide.

Once you have mastered the following simple exercise, you will be able to identify colors in your own and other people's auras by holding your hand above the head and shoulders and gradually moving in through the layers.

Experimenting with Psychometry, or Psychic Touch

Place in a box or container seven different-colored ribbons—red, orange, yellow, green, blue, indigo, and violet. Mix them, close your eyes, and pick one at a time, in turn, for a minute or two, describing on a voice recorder what each color feels like. Give each a number before describing it.

Keep the ribbons in order of feeling them or ask a friend to place them in order after picking each one, until you have picked them all up, and afterward check your sensations with your words.

Keep practicing using different-colored crystals, flowers, unlit candles, and food. You will find color identification even easier with organic materials.

Claircognizance, or Psychic Sensing

For the next stage, mix the ribbons with your eyes closed and keep them closed while placing them on a table, with a good space between each one so the energies don't mix. Again, if you wish, ask a friend to help you. It can be good learning about auras with another enthusiast.

This time, hold your hands a few inches (several cm) above each ribbon with your eyes closed, again using a recorder and giving each a number.

When you are confident using both techniques, add subsidiary colors that may also appear in the aura; brown is grounded and stable, pink is loving and nurturing, and gray is balanced and private.

TWENTY WAYS TO INSTANTLY IMPROVE YOUR AURA

1. Eat brightly colored fruits and vegetables, either raw or lightly cooked, to make your aura more radiant. Berries and raw peppers are instant aura energy lifters.

2. Go outdoors in natural light for a few minutes whenever possible if you work in a setting of constant artificial lighting, which is an aura drainer.

3. Work with a dish of mixed crystals in the different colors of the rainbow. When you wake up, pick one crystal without looking and hold it in your cupped hands. We are automatically drawn through the sensitive energy centers in our palms and fingertips to the most helpful crystal, and this will be the color your aura needs most.

4. If you feel hostility around you, move the palms of your hands together and outward again so they almost touch and then a few inches (several cm) apart, very slowly to build up the energy between them. When you feel your hands becoming heavy, move your hands quickly apart (it may be hard) and shake your fingers over your head and shoulders from above your hairline. This will create psychic sparks around your whole aura that will deter spite or hostility.

5. Keep a pot of growing fragrant flowers around your home or office to circulate and infuse your aura with health.

6.   On dark, cold days, wear at least one bright color to stimulate your aura and counteract the sleepy, dull energies that can sap enthusiasm.

7.   Make drinks with water in which you have soaked a blue lace agate, jade, or amethyst crystal for two or three hours, and offer it to critical or overactive people. It will blend their auras into harmony with yours. If it isn't possible for them to drink it, then drinking the water yourself will protect your aura against them.

8.   Drink plenty of water every day. Coffee, tea, carbonated drinks, and any drinks with additives can make the aura energy field dry and irritable.

9.   Gentle exercises, such as dancing, swimming, walking, or cycling, will help to circulate your aura energies even better than overly vigorous activities that may deplete reserves by causing energies to shoot out randomly in all directions.

10. Avoid excessive contact with synthetic materials and, whenever possible, wear natural fabrics next to the skin to avoid stifling your aura.

11. If you work with high-tech machinery or use a mobile phone or computer at home a lot, set green malachite or gray smoky quartz between you and the machine. Alternatively, keep a small crystal with your mobile phone to prevent it from sucking energy from your aura.

12. Pets are very good at transferring their loving, accepting energies from their aura to yours. As you stroke your pet, picture his soft brown, pink, and green energies overlaying your own like a gentle protective cover.

13. Send aura power to anyone in need, such as a child or a partner, even if she is absent, by holding a picture of her and, as you gently breathe, imagine a soft pink light enveloping her. This is good if the loved one is far away.

14. Keep pots of fresh herbs growing in your kitchen to spread a sense of abundance and to draw good things into the aura or energy field of your home.

15. Place wind chimes, bells, feathery plants, and mirrors around your home to keep the aura of the home lively and health-giving energies flowing.

16. Gold jewelry will fill your aura with confidence and focus, and is good if you need to impress others or show authority.

17. Silver jewelry will increase harmony and bring peace and reconciliation to any interaction.

18. Copper jewelry fills your aura with love, and will attract and increase love in your life.

19. If you feel totally exhausted or depressed, gently pass a clear quartz crystal pendulum or point in clockwise circles through your hair, then down over your eyebrows in clockwise circles, just touching the skin, then over your throat and your wrist points for your heart energies. This will give you a rapid infusion of power and enthusiasm.

20. When you need to sleep or rest, pass either an amethyst crystal pendulum or a crystal point counterclockwise in the same way to still your aura so you can rest and be restored.

In the first two chapters, we will learn the significance of different aura colors, not only to interpret the aura but to heal and cleanse it. This process will also bring aura harmony to a group of people at work or in a social gathering.

❖ 1 ❖

THE COLORS OF
THE AURA

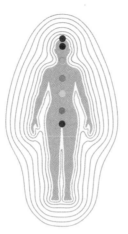

CHAPTERS I AND 2 CONTAIN ALL THE BASIC INFORMATION you need to interpret aura colors, as well as crystals, fragrances, and the archangels associated with them. That way, you can use them to cleanse, strengthen, and heal individual aura strands, as well as the whole aura. Each color has positive and negative connotations, according to its shade and clarity.

However, if you want to start reading auras now, go to Chapter 3 (page 27) and Chapter 4 (page 39) to learn different methods of aura interpretation. Return to Chapter 1 and Chapter 2 (page 15) as you work to check the meanings of the colors you sense or see.

In practice, once you have started to learn about aura color significance, you will suddenly become aware of one or two predominant colors around people. You will also spontaneously become aware of someone's mood, even if you see him approaching across a parking lot, by the colors you see or sense around him, especially around his head and shoulders.

By the same token, when you meet new people you will notice quite naturally that you can sum up their characters by the colors they radiate, and invariably you will be proven right. This can be useful in all kinds of situations, from meeting new family members to job interviews. Children can see auras automatically, so it is a question of relaxing and letting this ability come flooding back.

In supermarket checkout lines, at a concert, in a traffic jam, in a café, or when visitors come to the workplace, ask yourself if someone is a blue, red, green, or yellow person, and check the colors when you get home to see if they match with the person's behavior or words.

CHILDREN AND AURA COLORS

While most adults display two or three consistent aura colors to indicate their basic character and a more flickering transient overall color that changes with mood, babies begin with white or gold auras at birth and some midwives describe a golden light as the infant is born. If a birth is traumatic, the aura may temporarily be misty white.

By about a year old, as the child becomes more integrated into the world, she operates through the violet/indigo levels, which enable her to be very psychic, though this ability may gradually fade in the preschool years. At the same time, the newborn infant will also display the root level of red because of her total dependency on the caregiver to survive. The child will move into the needs and desires of the orange layer at about two years old and begin to learn the logic of yellow and mutually loving relationships of green by her early school days. For many children, access to the higher chakras disappears by age seven, but some retain it, together with their natural clairvoyance.

However, some very sensitive children retain a predominance of indigo in their auras and find the everyday world tough to navigate, as they don't like the noise; that is, the dishonesty of people who pretend to be what they are not. They may display educational problems, hyperactivity, even communication difficulties, such as Asperger's syndrome, because the world is out of sync with them and their less sensitive peers may tease and bully them.

Children are now occasionally born with complete rainbow auras, with all the colors bright and in balance, and it would seem they have come to bring peace to the world. Such babies are unusually alert, can see spirits and angels, can interact wonderfully with animals, and often are extraordinarily wise, with knowledge of past worlds from an early age.

THE SEVEN MAIN COLORS OF THE AURA

Red, orange, yellow, and green represent the inner earthly daily living and relationship aura levels, while blue, indigo, and violet reflect the higher spiritual levels. The colors move from red, which is closest to the body and well defined, to the diffuse seventh outermost layer, violet, which merges with the white and gold of the cosmos. I have included white in this chapter, as it is often seen as part of or suffusing the seventh layer. More cosmic and subsidiary colors are contained within or suffuse the separate bands I describe in the next chapter.

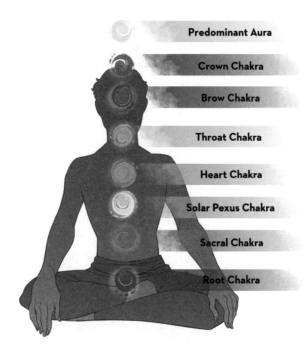

Predominant Aura

Crown Chakra

Brow Chakra

Throat Chakra

Heart Chakra

Solar Pexus Chakra

Sacral Chakra

Root Chakra

A LITTLE BIT OF AURAS

Red

For action, survival, change, power, physical energy, courage, determination, and passion; the color of the crusader.

Red forms the innermost aura layer.

POSITIVE QUALITIES: As clear bright red, scarlet, or rich ruby, it indicates vibrant life, the ability to overcome any obstacles, a desire to initiate positive change, and a passionate lover.

NEGATIVE QUALITIES: Bright metallic red signals a short temper, a bullying nature, a tendency to erupt if frustrated, and impulsivity or risk taking. When the red is dull or harsh, it reveals suppressed fury, an irritable nature, and resentment over perceived injustices, which build up rapidly. Scarlet-flashing auras suggest a flirtatious nature and maybe inappropriate passion.

ARCHANGEL: Camael, archangel of Mars, who rides his leopard to victory

FRAGRANCES: Cinnamon, cypress, dragon's blood, ginger, and mint

STRENGTHENING GEMS AND CRYSTALS: Blood agate, fire opal, heliotrope, garnet, jasper, meteorite, obsidian, red aventurine, red tigereye, and ruby

CHAKRA: Root or base

Orange

For confidence, independence, and a strong sense of identity, fertility, self-esteem, health, happiness, and personal desires; the color of the integrator.

Orange forms the second layer of the aura, moving out from the body.

POSITIVE QUALITIES: Warm, rich orange indicates the ability to integrate different aspects of life; sociability; self-motivation, originality, and creative abilities; and an open-minded, enthusiastic, and optimistic nature. Bright orange is an excellent sign for anyone wanting children.

NEGATIVE QUALITIES: A pale orange may indicate a lack or loss of identity or low self-esteem, someone who bases his sense of worth and identity only on what others think, or someone who is being bullied. Murky orange may indicate an oversensitive ego and territorial tendencies. Overly harsh orange represents excesses and obsessions, especially issues relating to food and self-image.

ARCHANGEL: Gabriel, archangel of the moon

FRAGRANCES: Eucalyptus, jasmine, lemon, and myrrh

STRENGTHENING GEMS AND CRYSTALS: Silver, moonstone, mother-of-pearl, pearl, opal, and selenite

CHAKRA: Sacral

Yellow

For logic and intellectual achievement, speculative abilities, versatility and mental dexterity, and changeability or restlessness. The color of the communicator and the traveler.

Yellow is the third level of the aura, moving outward, and one of the everyday living layers.

POSITIVE QUALITIES: Clear lemon yellow is the color of a focused mind and a sharp memory, of financial and business acumen, especially in speculation and technological expertise. Bright yellow is a color of joy and of clear communication, and brilliant canary yellow suggests a potential actor or entertainer. Clear yellowy brown augurs a scientific or mathematical mind.

NEGATIVE QUALITIES: Irregular harsh streaks of yellow indicate hyperactivity, while mustard yellow may mask jealousy or resentment. A metallic yellow haze conceals less-than-honest intent and a tendency toward gambling. Sharp lemon yellow may be logical but may also represent a sharp, sarcastic tongue. Mustard yellow may also indicate spite, or a potential gossip. A very cold yellow may suggest that the head always rules the heart.

ARCHANGEL: Raphael, archangel of healing, travel, and the entrepreneur

FRAGRANCES: Lavender, lily of the valley, melissa (lemon balm), lemongrass, and fennel

Calcite (yellow and honey calcite), chrysoberyl, lemon chrysoprase, citrine, jasper, rutilated quartz, and yellow topaz

CHAKRA: Solar plexus

Green

For love, fidelity, trust, harmony, natural growth in every way, and concern of the environment; the color of the child of nature.

Green is the fourth layer of the aura, moving outward, and the last daily life level. At its outer limits, it reflects love of humanity.

POSITIVE QUALITIES: Rich, clear green reveals a trustworthy, loving heart, who is generous with time, love, and money, and whose words come from the heart. A green aura is the sign of a person deeply committed in love. Emerald green shows a natural healer, especially in the alternative field, and someone who is naturally lucky.

NEGATIVE QUALITIES: Pale green suggests emotional dependency. A dull, muddy green can reveal conflicting emotions or a potential emotional vampire who sucks energy from others. Yellowy green can be a sign of possessiveness and emotional blackmail. Lime green may imply stress in current relationships. A cloudy or dark green aura may indicate those who love unwisely and too much, or who are pining for unrequited love.

ARCHANGEL: Anael, the archangel of lasting love, fidelity, and natural growth in any matter

FRAGRANCES: Apple blossom, lemon verbena, magnolia, and vanilla

STRENGTHENING GEMS AND CRYSTALS: Amazonite, aventurine, chrysoprase, emerald, fluorite, jade, malachite, moss agate, peridot, and tourmaline

CHAKRA: Heart

Blue

For ideals; broad vision, both of perspective and physical horizons; natural authority; and healing powers transmitted through higher sources; the color of the seeker of truth.

Blue is the first of the higher and outer aura levels and the fifth one, moving outward from the body.

POSITIVE QUALITIES: Royal blue indicates an integrated personality, with a keen sense of justice and natural powers of leadership. Bright blue is very creative and also altruistic. Pale blue is the color of the idealist with global vision. Clear blue represents objectivity, and the possessor is often a gifted speaker and teacher. Blue auras suffusing other aura colors can be seen around spiritual healers; authors; and musicians, actors, and other performers.

NEGATIVE QUALITIES: Dull, dense blue may represent increased conservatism and a concern for rigid rule keeping, regardless of circumstances. Harsh blue is a sign of someone who is autocratic, opinionated, and intolerant of others' lifestyles and beliefs.

ARCHANGEL: Sachiel, archangel of the harvest, truth, justice, prosperity, expansion in every way, and traditional learning

FRAGRANCES: Fennel, honeysuckle, lotus, sage and sagebrush, and sandalwood

STRENGTHENING GEMS AND CRYSTALS: Aqua aura, angelite, blue chalcedony, blue lace agate, blue quartz, celestite, cobalt aura, kyanite, iolite, lapis lazuli, sapphire, topaz, and turquoise

CHAKRA: Throat

Indigo

For inner vision and psychic awareness, spirituality, and knowledge of the future and of past lives/worlds; the color of the seer, the wise one, and the evolving soul.

Indigo forms the second of the higher levels of the aura and is the sixth layer, moving outward from the body. It often merges with the violet outermost layer.

POSITIVE QUALITIES: Clear indigo indicates acute sensitivity to people's unspoken intentions and awareness of the spiritual world, enhanced intuition, clairvoyance (psychic vision with the inner eye) and clairaudience (psychic hearing), and charitable care for all in need. The brighter shades indicate a fertile imagination. Deep indigo is present in the auras of wise older people. Lavender, which is a shade related to indigo, brings sensitivity to the higher powers within nature, and those with a lavender tinge in their aura enjoy an awareness of devas and a gift for herbalism.

NEGATIVE QUALITIES: When the indigo aura is blurred, it implies that its owner is spending too long on daydreams and illusions or on self-pity and a tendency to stress, especially absorbing other people's negative moods. A dark indigo indicates isolation and disillusionment with the world. An all-suffusing indigo can reveal a person with Asperger's syndrome or other conditions associated with oversensitivity to the world, especially among the young.

ARCHANGEL: Cassiel, archangel of consolation and compassion for the world's sorrows, who turns sorrow to joy and brings acceptance of what cannot be changed

FRAGRANCES: Mimosa, myrrh, mugwort, patchouli, and violet

STRENGTHENING GEMS AND CRYSTALS: Amethyst, ametrine, fluorite, kunzite, sodalite, super seven, and tanzanite

CHAKRA: Brow or third eye

Violet

For medium senses and connection with other dimensions and with ancestors, angels, and spirit guides; the color of the mystic, the visionary, and of integration between all aspects of the self and with the spiritual world.

Violet is the highest aura level and merges into white and gold, as it is joined to pure cosmic energies. White, especially, often forms part of this aura layer.

POSITIVE QUALITIES: A connection with unconscious wisdom and the collective knowledge of humankind in all places and ages. The ability to think laterally and globally and to disregard immediate gain to achieve a long-term goal; a love and tolerance of humanity with all its weaknesses and a peacemaker with the highest ethics; the ability to heal through higher energy sources, such as angels and wise guides; a tendency to gain recognition, especially in the performing or creative arts, in a meaningful rather than a merely commercial way.

NEGATIVE QUALITIES: When violet is too pale, drive, incentive, and stamina may be lacking, and grand plans rarely come to fruition. Too harsh a violet indicates perfectionism and/or an unrealistic idea of what is possible—that is, the inability to accept everyday life and people with all their imperfections. A dull violet may indicate depression.

ARCHANGEL: Zadkiel, angel of truth and justice, higher healing and abundance, the performing arts, and all alternative therapies and major charitable initiatives

FRAGRANCES: Bergamot, magnolia, lilies, orchids, and sweetgrass

STRENGTHENING GEMS AND CRYSTALS: Charoite, lepidolite, purpurite, purple spinel, sugilite, titanium aura, and violan

CHAKRA: Crown

White: The Predominant Higher-Aura Color

For limitless potential, boundless energy, the free-flowing life force, the color of the soaring spirit, the quester, and the innovator.

White often forms part of the outermost seventh aura layer in highly evolved people, especially where indigo and violet merge in the sixth aura layer, or white may overlay the violet. Indeed, from the sixth layer on, the colors become much more blended.

POSITIVE QUALITIES: At its most vibrant, this aura is the color of those who follow a unique life path and make a difference in the world. It draws pure, undiffused light from the cosmos that can be used for healing. It is a highly evolved color, indicating higher levels of consciousness, purity of intention, and the quest for what is of worth.

NEGATIVE QUALITIES: A pale, misty white may suggest a person who is out of touch with the real world and is involved in grandiose spiritual plans that have no foundation in reality. Murky white masks feelings of alienation and an unwillingness to reach out to others. An overly brilliant white heralds a holier-than-thou attitude and obsession with physical perfection and beauty; also, the drive to push ahead, regardless of the consequences to others, and eventual burnout.

ARCHANGELS: Michael, the archangel of the sun, and Gabriel, the archangel of the moon, for the synthesis of outer and inner worlds. The two archangels represent the synthesis of male and female energies. Michael has a male focus, and Gabriel has a female focus.

FRAGRANCES: Chamomile, copal, frankincense, and sunflowers

STRENGTHENING GEMS AND CRYSTALS: Clear aragonite, diamond, clear fluorite, clear crystal quartz, herkimer diamond, opal aura, rainbow quartz, white sapphire, white topaz, and zircon

CHAKRA: The crown chakra, extending from the center of the hairline on the upper forehead to about an inch (2-3 cm) above the head, where it merges with the minor but significant soul star chakra that contains the unchanging divine spark of our evolved or higher spiritual self

In the next chapter we will look at the meanings of higher-vibration colors and subsidiary colors that are often perceived in the aura.

❧ 2 ❧

MORE AURA
COLORS

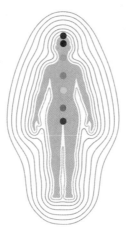

LIKE THE WHITE AURA COLOR, WHICH WE FOCUSED ON IN Chapter 1, gold, magenta, turquoise, and silver are also higher-aura colors, linking the seven color aura bands with higher dimensions and the cosmos. In an exceptionally wise or holy person, these higher shades may suffuse the whole aura. Other subsidiary colors form variations of the seven main colors, but they may flood their related aura band if they are particularly strong. For example, in the case of a new mother, human or animal, pink—which we will touch on later in this chapter—may fill the whole aura in the days and weeks after birth.

Gold

For perfection, and for striving to achieve high and worthwhile goals. The color of the visionary and of achieving fame or greatness in furthering the good of humanity or stretching the boundaries of possibility; also the color of the pioneer, the adventurer, and all who live a truly good life.

It is rare, outside of a saint or a great humanitarian leader, to see a completely gold aura. Typically, gold appears as tiny shimmers or a thin band radiating with stars on the outermost edge of the outermost layer of the aura, merging above the white with the cosmos.

POSITIVE QUALITIES: Though a new baby will be surrounded by gold, this soon fades, but you can be sure that if a child retains gold in the aura, she is destined to be a very special person. Gold is the color of one who will become wealthy or famous but will use that wealth and fame for the good of others and will change the world in a positive way. A single gold star on top of the head indicates special talents that can open the doors of the future.

NEGATIVE QUALITIES: A harsh gold indicates an obsession with power and a desire for worldly wealth at any cost. A tarnished gold may suggest a tendency toward addictions, obsessions, and compulsions.

ARCHANGEL: Michael, archangel of the sun, the angel who favors personal and unique enterprise and guides all who have a unique destiny

FRAGRANCES: Chamomile, copal, frankincense, marigold, orange, and sunflower

STRENGTHENING GEMS AND CRYSTALS: Gold, boji stones, chalcopyrite, clear quartz crystal, diamond, polished iron pyrites, tigereye, golden topaz

CHAKRA: The whole chakra system

OTHER HIGHER COLORS IN THE AURA

Magenta

For spirituality expressed in the everyday world, for originality of vision, and for a path of service to others; the color of the teacher of truth and the release of the pain and suffering of others.

Magenta can be a band at the top of the violet layer or even between the indigo and violet. If a person is very evolved and dedicated to passing on wisdom and healing to those who need it, magenta may suffuse the whole aura at times.

POSITIVE QUALITIES: Rich magenta is the color of spiritual leaders, whether a teacher of reiki or a great guru. It is most often seen in the aura of the wise one who has acquired wisdom through suffering and has used that experience for the benefit of others. However, it can also be seen in much younger people and any who have battled back from serious illness or who refuse to let disability or the impending threat of mortality defeat them.

NEGATIVE QUALITIES: An overly harsh magenta belongs to the false guru or those who use spiritual power to dominate others. It also characterizes those who are so inflated by their own spiritual knowledge that they lose sight of the truth.

ARCHANGEL: Metatron, who, though he is described as a shimmering pillar of light, is the archangel of transformation, with his pen and scroll. He was transformed through thunder and lightning from the mortal prophet Enoch.

FRAGRANCES: Frankincense, juniper, lemongrass, myrrh, orchid, and sandalwood

STRENGTHENING GEMS AND CRYSTALS: Blue aventurine, flint, mahogany obsidian, meteorite, sardonyx, tektite, and titanium aura

CHAKRA: Third eye/brow chakra, connected also with the crown

Turquoise

For integration of heart and mind, feelings and thoughts, and the synthesis of wisdom and experience; the color of the wise healer.

Turquoise originates in the fourth (green) and the fifth (blue) layers of the aura, moving outward from the head as these two bands of color merge.

It may suffuse the aura in a mystic, an aid worker, an artist, a writer, or an inventor, and it indicates an old soul.

POSITIVE QUALITIES: Clear, bright turquoise represents impartiality and justice, mingled with compassion. Clear turquoise indicates an unwavering devotion to friends and family, and anyone in need, in good times and bad. He is a potential counselor, negotiator, orator, and arbitrator, and in public or personal life inspires devotion and respect. However, turquoise people are not personally ambitious or success-oriented, but believe in what they do.

NEGATIVE QUALITIES: An overly harsh turquoise aura indicates a charismatic person who uses her gifts to win favor from the influential for personal status and glory.

ARCHANGEL: Sandalphon, the twin of Metatron, once the prophet Elijah, who ascended to the heavens in a chariot of fire and, like Metatron, is an angel of transformation and traditional wisdom

FRAGRANCES: Lilies, lotus, mint, musk, all fragrant roses, sandalwood, and thyme

STRENGTHENING GEMS AND CRYSTALS: Aquamarine, bornite or peacock ore, and cobalt and titanium—which are metals bonded with quartz—as well as chrysocolla, lapis lazuli, opal, and turquoise

CHAKRA: Heart/throat, and the minor chakra, the thymus chakra below the base of the neck

Silver

Represents dreams, magic, visions, and a desire for fulfillment beyond the material world; the ability to travel between the dimensions and connect with extraterrestrial worlds, sudden insights, especially in dreams, meditation and daytime visions, the color of the dreamer.

Associated with the second orange layer of the aura and also spread around the whole aura as stars or streaks in the higher-aura layers.

POSITIVE QUALITIES: Pure silver is often seen around a parent who has given a great deal to the family, perhaps because of a child's disability. Silver stars or sparks in an aura indicate hidden spiritual potential, and may also appear around the time a woman is about to conceive a child; it remains throughout pregnancy and childbirth. However, silver can equally refer to the seeds of imagination and creativity that may be developed and awakening or reawakening sexuality. Silver stars are also the mark of a gifted teacher.

NEGATIVE QUALITIES: Metallic flashes throughout the aura are a sign of someone who is seeking to create an illusion or image, or craves excitement and stimulation by dubious means and who will take risks.

ARCHANGEL: Gabriel, archangel of the Moon

FRAGRANCES: Cherry, jasmine, lemon verbena, poppy, rose, and ylang-ylang

STRENGTHENING GEMS AND CRYSTALS: Hematite, mica, moonstone, mother-of-pearl, pearl, rainbow moonstone, selenite, silver, and white opal

CHAKRA: Heart and sacral

SUBSIDIARY CHAKRAS WITHIN THE SEVEN AURA BANDS

Pink

For unconditional love, reconciliation, practical nurturing and gentleness; the color of the wise counselor and unconditional love.

Pink forms part of the green aura band, but may suffuse the aura of girls reaching puberty, and anyone experiencing first love or the regrowth of trust. It is seen around pregnant women and new mothers, as well as pregnant animals and animal mothers.

POSITIVE QUALITIES: Bright pink is the color of the peacemaker between friends, family, and colleagues; the mender of bruised or broken hearts; and the healer of emotional sorrows and abuse. Gentle, kind, patient, and tolerant of others' failings, the clear pink person always sees the best in everyone; she's a loyal friend who makes any home beautiful and who is excellent with children and young animals. Clear pink also suggests fertility.

NEGATIVE QUALITIES: A very pale pink, seen in men and women, is the little boy or girl lost syndrome, who constantly seeks rescuing. A dull or murky/muddy pink aura can indicate a "poor me" martyrdom attitude. A very misty pink reveals that the possessor sees other people's point of view so much that he will take the path of least resistance and won't stand up for justice.

ARCHANGEL: Ariel, lioness of God

FRAGRANCES: Apple blossom, cherry blossom, geranium, lilac, melissa (lemon balm), pink roses, and vanilla

STRENGTHENING GEMS AND CRYSTALS: Coral, kunzite, mangano or pink calcite, morganite, pink chalcedony, opal, rose quartz, and tourmaline

CHAKRA: Heart

Brown

For practical abilities, stability and reliability, love of animals, acceptance of frailty in self and others, and earth-related power; the color of the builder of firm foundations.

Brown relates to the lower, slower vibrations of the innermost red band.

POSITIVE QUALITIES: Rich, golden brown shows a person deeply rooted in Mother Earth, a keen environmentalist and lover of the land, a doer rather than a thinker, a natural homemaker and home lover, and someone gifted at arts and crafts, home renovation, and gardening. A dark brown shows wise caution with finances and property, and sympathy toward older people.

NEGATIVE QUALITIES: Murky brown can indicate narrow horizons, increased cautiousness, and a prejudiced outlook, someone who can be stingy with money and finds it hard to show affection. A harsh brown is the aura of someone who is obsessed with money or material concerns and who is a workaholic. Very pale brown appears when someone is overburdened by practical or financial worries.

ARCHANGEL: Cassiel, archangel of Saturn in his practical, cautious, boundary-setting aspects

FRAGRANCES: Hibiscus, mimosa, patchouli, sweetgrass, tea tree, and thyme

STRENGTHENING GEMS AND CRYSTALS: Bronzite, desert rose, leopardskin or snakeskin jasper, rutilated quartz, all the sand-colored and brown mottled jaspers, and tigereye

CHAKRA: Root or base, also with the minor earth star chakra located around the ankles, sides, and soles of the feet

Gray

The color of compromise, adaptability, and the ability to merge into the background; the color of the keeper of secrets and of mystery.

Gray is a lower part of the innermost red aura, but it can also sometimes emanate from the yellow third band as mist covering the whole aura, when a person is trying to avoid revealing her thoughts and intentions.

POSITIVE QUALITIES: A silvery dove-gray is an aura that expresses neutrality and a wish to avoid emotional or controversial matters or make a commitment. A clear gray is good at making things happen behind the scenes. Gray-aura people are hard to get to know, as they tend to be all things to all people. They rarely make a fuss and are natural detectives and spies.

NEGATIVE QUALITIES: A dull gray may suggest depression and, around the knee area, may show a person holding on to grief. A very pale gray can be a symbol of indecision and indicate a fence sitter. A foggy, dense gray is generally a "keep out" aura, usually because there is something to hide (be wary of this in a new lover) and a lack of principles. A murky gray aura indicates hidden information or half-truths that may suggest you should be cautious in trusting this person without safeguards.

ARCHANGEL: Raziel, angel of divine mysteries and secrets, credited with writing the esoteric Book of the Angel Raziel, containing all earthly and heavenly knowledge; often described as an outline behind a dark gray, semitransparent curtain

FRAGRANCES: Ambergris, cedar, lavender, lemon verbena, sweet marjoram, myrrh, musk, and patchouli

STRENGTHENING GEMS AND CRYSTALS: Apache tears, fossils, grey banded agate, iron pyrites, laboradite, smoky quartz, tektite, and turritella agate

CHAKRA: Root or solar plexus

Black

For transitions, rest leading to regeneration, sorrows, and obstacles to be overcome.

Though black is the lowest part of the innermost aura layer, it can appear anywhere in the aura, especially as knots or tangles, and indicates the need for attention in that particular area, especially emotionally.

POSITIVE QUALITIES: A clear black, almost transparent aura may indicate that a person is resting emotionally and spiritually, perhaps after an exhausting or stressful period or after bereavement, and needs time to grow stronger behind the protective darkness. Because psychic protection is so strongly implicated in a positive black aura, someone with a black aura may deliberately or spontaneously be shielding herself from intrusion . . . so this is not an aura to try to read.

NEGATIVE QUALITIES: A matte black indicates exhaustion or depression and is more often seen as black spots or streaks than as a blanket aura. However, a harsh metallic black can suggest that the person is potentially a psychic or an emotional vampire or has serious addictions or criminal tendencies. This is an aura to avoid unless you are a very experienced healer.

ARCHANGEL: Cassiel, angel of serenity. Cassiel teaches us calmness and stillness, enabling thought and careful consideration before taking action

FRAGRANCES: Myrrh, musk, and mugwort

STRENGTHENING GEMS AND CRYSTALS: Obsidian, smoky quartz, and Apache tear, all of which are translucent

CHAKRA: Root or base, and minor earth star

In the next chapter, we will work with the dominant transient mood aura that indicates the way people are feeling and are likely to react.

✦ 3 ✦

EXPLORING THE MOOD AURA

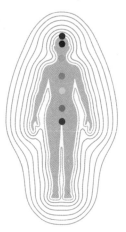

HUMAN AURAS ARE CONSTANTLY CHANGING. OUR AURAS are affected both positively and negatively by the energy fields of other people with whom we interact and the physical, mental, and emotional environment in which we live and work. These mood auras can also be influenced by memories of past situations and fears, or anticipation about the future.

Some people are prone to rapid mood swings and are especially sensitive to external events and inner thoughts. The auras of hyperactive and ADHD children, or those with Asperger's syndrome, are wide open and therefore are easily affected by unfriendly peers and insensitive adults. Others on the autistic spectrum have closed their auras at a very early age to avoid the intense pain of interactions with the world in general—the good as well as the bad.

Being able to instantly read the mood auras of individuals and, with practice, groups of people at work or in social situations tells you what is going on, even under the surface, and puts you one step ahead.

Throughout the day, situations and people may not only temporarily affect your aura color, but, if you feel strongly or are concentrating hard, one mood color will flood the whole aura. For example, if you were fully concentrating on learning something new, a clear yellow would predominate. If you were working on your spiritual development, one of the higher-aura bands, such as indigo, would temporarily suffuse the seven aura bands, even for a while covering the ever-present stable personality or permanent aura I will describe in the next chapter.

These temporary colors tend to flicker and be quite transient and, when you first learn to read the aura, the mood will usually be the first and clearest color you see, since it is fueled by emotion and so easily spreads throughout the whole energy field.

This has been the case time and time again when I have worked with people, interpreting the images created by an aura camera. An aura camera converts the predominant aura colors into a printed image of a head-and-shoulders view. It works when an individual puts his hands on metal plates as he sits in front of the aura camera.

If one color predominates at the time of the photograph, it will be because that color reflects the immediate strong mood being felt by the person and so blots out all the others. For example, I watched a couple standing near an aura camera having an argument, because the man said the photo would be a waste of money. His partner snapped back, saying he was mean and always stopped her from having fun. The woman was still fuming when she sat for her picture, and refused to calm down before having it taken. As a result, the photograph displayed a harsh red color all over the aura, spilling out to the edges of the picture. Her partner had stormed off, so, regrettably, I could not see his aura picture. Do a quick review of the previous two chapters and figure out what you would have expected his mood color to be.

IDENTIFYING THE MOOD AURA

When you see this aura, it will be quite sparkly. You will probably initially see the mood aura color in your mind. If you are very logical, your mind may initially block even this process. In this case, say or write the first color that comes into your mind as you look at the person, for that invariably reflects her correct mood aura.

Begin by programming your psychic eye and intuitive senses by saying aloud or in your mind, *First I wish to focus on the mood aura.*

Look either directly toward the subject or, if it would be impolite to stare if she is close, somewhere over her left or right shoulder, whichever is easier. You might even look at her from the back view, as the aura extends all around the body for an arm span or more at its brightest. The head and shoulders give you the clearest view.

Slowly close your eyes and just as slowly open them and blink. You should instantly *see* the mood aura.

Whether you see the colors in your mind or externally, the mood texture will be slightly more ethereal than the physical body. The

mood texture will resemble finely woven, colored, sparkly, net curtain material, moving quite fast all the time, like shallow water rippling over sand or sunlight dancing on water.

If the mood aura fades before you have processed the information, repeat the exercise. The mood aura color should remain in your
mind for longer. The mood aura may increase or decrease in size and
intensity, even within less than a minute.

Your psychic sensing or claircognizant abilities (also called the
sixth sense or, by Scottish people, *kenning*) will kick in quite early.

If the mood aura is pale or, conversely, very harsh, you may
sense sudden exhaustion and defeat in your own body, perhaps
because the person whose aura you're reading is being bullied by
a colleague or partner, or you may feel a grating in your teeth, like
biting on ice, if the person you are studying is about to shout down
someone else.

If a child consistently comes home from school with a pale mood
aura, make tactful inquiries if he is being teased, even if you see no
outward signs of physical harm.

Remember, a mood need not be caused by a present event; sometimes an old memory can intrude and flood us with sorrow or joy.
You will intuitively sense, given practice, the time frame of the event
causing the mood color, whether current, recalled, anticipated, or
feared. This intuitive interpretation is possible because all impressions, images, and words spoken are stored in our aura, including
anger, passion, memories, and future fears. As you learn more about

the aura, you will be able to accurately pinpoint these moods and apply the necessary remedy to counteract any negativity.

If you yourself have seemingly inexplicable mood changes, see if you can link the timing of those changes to a similar situation in the past. If the mood is not positive, once you know the cause of the mood, in yourself or in others, you can then take action to say the right thing, offer support, steer clear of the trigger of discomfort, or work with an antidote color (introduced in Chapter 6, page 61).

Monitoring Your Own Mood Aura

Assess your own mood aura when you get up and at regular intervals during the day and evening. You will need a mirror or any reflective surface to do this. Experiment to see whether a darker or a lighter background is more helpful for you. You only need to see your head and shoulders.

Check in the bathroom mirror at work and, if the mood color is not positive, splash water over your hairline and your brow to cleanse your whole aura.

If your aura is close to your body, you may be feeling defensive. Keep in mind that the whole aura can move close to the body. Later we will learn how to deliberately withdraw the aura as a means of defense.

Record what was happening around the time you checked your aura and you may find a pattern of events or people that triggers a negative mood change or even drains you of your aura so it becomes very pale, and holes appear; for example, when you're in the presence of an emotional vampire. Though you may not be consciously aware of this, you will feel the effects of aura attack for hours or days afterward, whether this attack was deliberate or just an interaction with a natural leech or pessimistic soul. By anticipating the cause, you can then minimize the impact of such events or meetings, or shield your aura in advance.

Conversely, be attuned to happy situations and people who fill your aura with happiness or peace, and try to incorporate more of such encounters in your daily life.

Are there any people or events whose expected arrival prompts a strong positive or negative mood aura reaction? These can hold vital clues of which you may not have been aware; for example, you may no longer enjoy meeting a friend with whom you spend every Wednesday evening. Maybe you would rather go to the gym or stay at home.

Recording Your Findings

For a few weeks, practice identifying the mood aura in different people at work, at home, at the gym, at school, on the train, at the airport, or waiting in a supermarket checkout line. To check your findings, whenever possible, ask the person whose aura you read how she is feeling.

Make up an aura study folder by buying a loose-leaf folder and writing your findings on blank white paper as you continue to monitor the mood. Once you read later chapters, write down other aura aspects as well.

Create a page for each of the colors in the aura, including higher and subsidiary colors, based on Chapters 1 and 2 (page 1 and 15, respectively). Each time you come across a color, whether in the mood aura or another aura aspect, note what you felt and *saw*, and the circumstances that gave rise to the aura color in that particular shade. Then build up your own roster of color significances.

Record your findings using a head shape, as shown, that contains the seven layers.

Draw seven equal-sized circles around the head. As you become more experienced, you may notice that the mood aura not only affects and obscures the innermost everyday levels, but at times may disturb or enhance the outer layers as well.

Make your observations increasingly detailed, noting in writing at the side of the diagram how a scarlet temper aura becomes patchy during a toddler or teenage temper tantrum, for example, as the angry person pauses to see if the outburst is getting the desired effect.

Over the next few weeks, compare the situations and ages of people where you see, for example, that temper aura in a two-year-old or a boss raging because a deadline has not been met. See what conclusions you draw and how you would deal with each person. In Chapter 6, we will learn how to use antidote colors for such an event.

Some people, when they first begin to study auras, notice, while focusing on the mood aura, that beneath the mood color (like seeing layers of clouds from a plane), two or three colors are consistently bright but matte and not moving. This is true for yourself or others with whom you regularly interact. These will be the basic personality or permanent aura colors you perceive. As we noted earlier, they may extend beyond their own layers if they are powerful traits or during certain times in life.

However, if you see only the mood color at first, color all the bands in that shade. I will show you how to bring the personality aura into clear focus in Chapter 4.

In time, you will be creating a very detailed seven-band diagram that will tell you all you need to know for cleansing, healing, and strengthening the aura.

While you will use the basic color meanings, spelled out in Chapters 1 and 2, to help you understand the meanings of the mood aura, always trust your intuition and your feelings to guide you to the significance of an individual's feelings and thoughts. The more accurate you prove you are by your daily observations, the more confidence you will develop in your ability.

In a work situation, notice if the arrival or the anticipated arrival of a particular person in the office—for example, a visitor from the head office or the boss's wife or husband—affects everyone's mood aura in the same way or if they react differently.

Study the individual mood auras of a group of people on a Monday morning, before a weekend, before an official holiday, when they're under deadline pressure, and at a meeting or lecture. Focus on who is concentrating on the matter at hand, who is daydreaming, and what might be distracting them. The mood aura will give you clues; for example, sparkling green indicates straying thoughts of a tryst with a lover afterward.

On a Monday morning, observe the aura as each person enters the workplace and, where possible, inquire what each one did over the weekend. On a midweek day, you may be able to correlate an extra rush getting children off to school or an issue at home with the current mood aura. You can do the same with parents dropping off their children at school. Make casual remarks to elicit whether it has been a difficult morning so far or the person is feeling excited about a forthcoming event.

At a birthday party, a retirement party, a wedding, or a family celebration, note whose mood auras contradict their words and actions or the expected pleasure of the occasion and in what way (boredom, irritability, jealousy, concealed passion for the bride-groom). We will work on this in detail in Chapter 7, which focuses on aura interactions.

Observe fellow passengers on a plane to see who fears flying (a very harsh flickering red that indicates a desire to escape). The results may surprise you.

If you sit next to someone on a train or bus, assess his mood aura and then try to get him chatting about the reason for his journey.

Choose four, five, or six subjects to study in-depth over several weeks—maybe a few colleagues at work, and a family member or two—and note their mood colors at different times of the day and week. If a friend always visits her in-laws on a Tuesday, note how her mood aura changes not only the day after but the afternoon before.

After seeing the aura of the subjects of your in-depth studies, try to tune into the events that caused the aura. If possible, pick up a pen and let the words flow. Because you know the subjects, it is easier to tactfully question them about their feelings. The more you relax, the more easily this information will intuitively come to you.

If you see a relative, partner, neighbor, or colleague coming up the path or across the parking lot, quickly read and anticipate her mood. You can also do this if you are meeting someone for lunch, on an interviewing panel, or after work.

In the following chapter, we will work with the more permanent personality aura and add more colors to your seven-layer diagram.

❖ 4 ❖

UNDERSTANDING THE PERSONALITY AURA

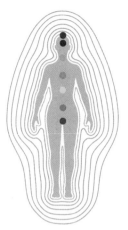

THE PERSONALITY AURA HELPS YOU UNDERSTAND WHAT makes people tick. It gives insight into the kind of people they are and the things that matter to them. As a result, you'll figure out the right approach to take in dealing with them. You may have already noticed one, two, or occasionally three areas of matte color behind the flickering mood aura. Personality auras are more static and smoother. In babyhood through early childhood, the personality aura changes rapidly. During the teen years and the early twenties, you can also see speedy changes in the personality aura, though the core color will remain the same or only slightly modified.

In adulthood, alterations in personality aura colors are brought about by major life-changing events. So, for example, falling deeply in love (emerald green), giving birth to a child (pink), and studying or having a gift for spirituality (indigo) will cause dramatic alteration in a relatively short time. By contrast, being deeply hurt by a betrayal in love can, almost overnight, put up dark or harsh color barriers

IDENTIFYING THE ASPECTS OF THE AURA YOU MOST NEED

In Chapter 3, we concentrated solely on the mood aura. Now the more permanent personality aura will fill your focus. Think of it as changing lenses on an expensive camera to focus on what you need to capture most.

Eventually, you will spontaneously sense or see all seven aura colors to read auras for personal information, rather than to heal. You will focus on mood and personality predominantly and bring these into sharper focus.

If you want to *see* the personality aura directly after you have studied the mood, wait a few moments, close your eyes, and rest all your psychic senses by picturing a deep blue velvet cloth in your mind.

The mood aura will automatically recede and, as you open your eyes, the personality aura color(s) will slowly replace the mood aura colors in your psychic vision. We'll probe the techniques for seeing or sensing the personality aura strands later in this chapter.

THE IMPORTANCE OF UNDERSTANDING THE PERSONALITY AURA

As you increasingly trust your findings, you may sometimes discover a surprising mismatch, such as a person who does not seem to enjoy her job no matter how good she is at it. As an example, you may find an indigo accountant or a lemon-yellow child-care worker, who, later in life, changed their career, from one they originally adopted to please parents or because it seemed like the sensible option. If you work as a therapist or in human resources, personality aura reading is a valuable skill to understand dilemmas that have no apparent cause.

However, that indigo accountant may be very intuitive, knowing instantly where issues or mistakes lie, and being popular with clients because of a gentle encouraging manner. The child-care worker might also be excellent at organization and seeing that every child is safely cared for.

When going on interviews, you can quickly understand not only the mood of the interviewers but the core values that they consider important. Whether you're out at a singles event, meeting colleagues at a new job or a training course, going to a social event with a partner, or meeting a partner's family for the first time, you instantly become aware of the right approach and topics that are safe to broach.

In time, you will be able to *read* personality auras by voice, by speaking on the telephone, or even by viewing online dating photographs.

STUDYING THE PERSONALITY AURA IN DETAIL

Those who have just one color in their personality aura tend to be very definite, fixed characters whose opinions are not easily shaken. However, if the personality aura is a pale, faded color, the person may have been emotionally or physically abused at some point in his life and has withdrawn from expressing opinions or even likes and dislikes.

Techniques to See the Personality Aura

Work initially with subjects you know well until you feel confident in your aura-reading skills. Then try reading the personality auras of strangers or acquaintances who come into work or whom you see socially, perhaps at the gym, so you can gain some feedback from tactful questioning about their lifestyle and preferences.

As with studying the mood aura, program your psychic eye by asking it to show you the personality aura and that alone.

Look toward your subject, but this time do not stare.

Gaze through half-closed eyes and the softer, smooth matte personality aura may spontaneously appear. If not, close your eyes as slowly as possible and open them just as slowly, but do not blink. The personality aura should remain present for a minute or two, or even longer. If not, repeat closing your eyes and opening them slowly and smoothly. You may, as you become more experienced, be aware of the mood aura in the background flickering behind the personality aura.

As with the mood aura, if you cannot see anything internally or externally, name or write down the color(s) you sense without pausing. This will cut through any unconscious blocks.

Recording the Personality Aura

When you record your findings in your seven-band diagram, color and label the diagram according to what you see and the relative positions of the colors, as a new personality aspect may be emerging.

In all likelihood, the personality aura color(s) will fill most or all the seven bands. However, sometimes the personality aura only covers the outer layers of the diagram, or each remains within its own related color strand. If this happens, especially if these color strands are not next to each other, it may be that the personality is being suppressed by circumstance or denying the true self. This can be confirmed if, for example, there is pale green in the fourth naturally green heart band moving outward, which suggests the person is living through others.

The relative positions of the colors is significant in assessing the predominant nature of the person, as one color may totally obscure the other(s). Alternatively, there may be a thin band of a subsidiary color farther out toward the cosmos, indicating it has not yet been awakened but could hold the key to happiness.

The closer a personality color is to the head or crown chakra, the more it manifests in daily life. And if you see evenly sized bands, the person is going to be balanced in different aspects of her personality, perhaps logic and creativity or work and home interests.

If the personality of the person is especially dominant, the personality aura color(s) may spill over the bands into the space around the bands. This is often true of single personality aura colors, such as the autocratic, rigid, dark blue.

Have a good selection of pencils, crayons, or marker pens on hand. Choose a set that has at least three shades that are widely available for each color.

AN ALTERNATIVE APPROACH TO AURA READING

If the methods suggested so far aren't working for you, consider the following methods, which draw on psychometry, or psychic touch.

First, take your time and go over the exercises of observation described so far in this and the previous chapter.

Alternatively, try the following technique, which will have you almost immediately identifying mood and personality auras if you are experiencing any blocks.

As suggested earlier, use a set of pencils, crayons, colored marker pens, or paints so that there are at least three shades for each color and a set of sparkly ones for the mood aura. Choose sparkly ones that have different shades for the same color, since the mood aura does sparkle as it comes into view. I found mine in the children's stationery section of the local supermarket.

We have minor chakras or psychic energy points in both hands, most specifically in the center of the palms. These chakras are connected to the heart chakra center through which psychic knowledge is channeled. Therefore, the technique of coloring spontaneously is a good way of recording what the physical eye misses.

Choose a subject who is going to stay relatively still for a while.

You don't have to know the person. You could sit in a park or a city square, watching someone eating lunch while reading or using a mobile phone. You could also study someone sitting on the other side of the office who is talking on the telephone.

Sit so you can see the head, front, or back of your subject, if possible framed against a soft light.

For both mood and personality aura observations, relax and let your eyes go into soft focus, as when you are daydreaming or drifting into sleep, so the person you are observing becomes almost blurred. Some people find it easier to look slightly to the side of the figure, rather than having him in the center of your vision. Alternatively, gaze a few inches (several cm) over his shoulder.

This time, just draw a circle to represent the subject's head on white paper, and around the outside of the head draw an inner circle for the personality aura and beyond the inner circle an outer circle for the mood aura.

Then, selecting crayons by touch, rather than looking in the box, color in the mood aura on the head diagram.

Switch your glance from the person to the page and back again, slowly and continuously, but do not try to control what your hand is doing. Flow with the coloring.

If none of the sparkly colors feels right for the mood aura as you touch them, try the personality color crayons that are more matte, as the mood aura may be dull, exhausted, or depressed.

You can then study and record the personality aura shade(s) in the same way, allowing the relative thickness of the bands, if more than one color, to appear spontaneously. Remember to close your eyes and allow the blue velvet curtain to enter your mind before switching to the personality aura.

THE NEXT STAGE IN AURA READING

Now we are going to combine mood and personality aura readings and add to what you already have learned in order to elicit more detail. Start a file on different people you regularly observe, and each time begin by studying the mood aura followed by the personality aura.

You are going to look at the two aura aspects in greater detail to observe psychically any dark streaks, such as holes or tangles that are within the aura strands, whether mood or personality.

For now, continue to draw the head as a circle and record the personality aura as the inner circle around the head (the colors may overlap) and the mood aura as a second outer circle around the personality circle.

This time you aren't going to deliberately stare or blink, though if you want to blink or close your eyes momentarily, that is fine. The key is not to force any impressions on yourself in any way.

This time, choose the colors consciously.

Study the mood aura first, using the method I suggested on page 29, then close your eyes and envision that blue velvet curtain. Then study the personality aura, using the technique on page 42.

This time, besides recording the actual colors and shades, mark any jagged lines, knots, tangles, dark streaks, pale areas, or even holes of which you become aware. These may indicate emotional traumas.

For example, a trigger marked by a tangle in the mood aura may cause a reaction not appropriate to the actual situation. The source may be an old put-down that makes any criticism unacceptable.

You may also hear in your mind words or phrases that add even more information about the aura and the person you are studying, so scribble these down on your diagram as well.

When you sense that there is no more information coming your way, label the picture with the setting, date, and, if you know it, the name of the person. If you do know the person, you may be able to match some of the information gained from the aura with the actual circumstances. But this is not as important as the practice at this stage.

ONGOING PERSONALITY AURA PRACTICE

Read personality auras everywhere, even if you cannot get feedback. With someone you are able to talk to (and it is remarkably easy to make casual conversation), read her personality aura.

See if the aura-strand colors of the loving parent (rich pink) and the stressed executive (overly bright blue) are balanced, or if there are any muddy colors that might suggest conflict of interest.

To record these extra details clearly, create a diagram of the head surrounded by two circles. In the first circle, record the mood aura; in the second one, record the personality aura. As you become familiar and experienced with auras, a more complicated diagram featuring seven circles—one for each aura layer—may be of more use in healing and cleansing work.

In the next chapter, we will work on cleansing and healing the aura and working with antidote colors.

CLEANSING, HEALING, AND ENERGIZING AURAS

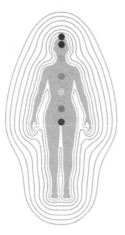

A S YOU HAVE STUDIED THE MOOD AND PERSONALITY auras, you may have already become aware of other aura color bands in the background.

These seven color bands, and the subsidiary colors within them, hold the key to health and well-being, and through them you can cleanse and energize the whole aura. You can also heal and strengthen individual aspects of it that cause the body, mind, and soul to be out of balance.

If the aura becomes blocked, overactive, or weakened, the effects may eventually bring on conditions to which a person has a predisposition, or it may exacerbate existing physical problems. For example, stress is often reflected in the aura as jaggedness or tangles and can eventually create illnesses or encourage existing ones.

With their permission, you can cleanse, heal, and empower the auras of friends and family or clients. If it is someone who is ill, ask if he would welcome a healing. It will be accepted if it is meant to be.

HOW TO IDENTIFY THE DIFFERENT AURA BANDS

The seven bands appear as a rainbow halo around the body in the shape of an ellipse but, again, they form most clearly around the head and shoulders.

Ask your psychic vision to show all seven strands to you, just as you did with the mood and personality auras in earlier activities. Relax and look through half-closed eyes, if necessary slowly closing and opening your eyes two or three times as you look at yourself in a mirror, or around the head and shoulders of the person you are going to help.

The Seven Aura Layers

Each aura layer is empowered by and, in turn, empowers a chakra, the invisible energy centers within our body. Each aura layer reflects the color of its chakra. The effects of blocked or overactive chakras are reflected in the aura layers and can be healed or strengthened by working directly with the aura. The aura colors spill out from the inner spiritual body of which the chakras are a part.

1. THE ETHERIC LAYER: THE INNERMOST LAYER OF THE AURA

This first aura layer is powered by the red base, or root, chakra energy center. Brown, black, and gray aura colors emanate from this chakra.

This red aura layer reflects your basic instincts and your overall physical health. It encompasses your flight-or-fight mech-

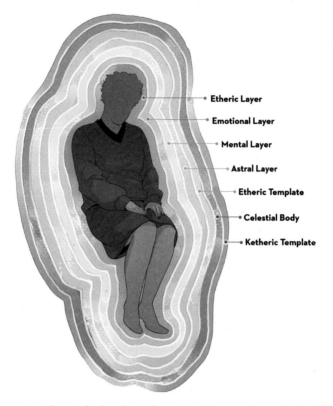

Etheric Layer

Emotional Layer

Mental Layer

Astral Layer

Etheric Template

Celestial Body

Ketheric Template

anisms, together with the physical stamina that energizes the body. Uncontrolled anger and aggression, and its more positive side—keen awareness of opportunity and danger, and survival mechanisms—reside here.

The etheric aura layer, like the base or root chakra, rules the legs, feet, and skeleton. This includes the teeth, joints, muscles, the cell structure, the bowels, the prostate, the circulatory system, and the large intestine.

2. THE EMOTIONAL LAYER: THE SECOND LAYER OF THE AURA

The second layer of the aura is powered by the orange sacral chakra. The aura at this level appears as orange light or silver, especially when sexual or fertility matters figure prominently in a person's life.

This is the layer of the aura that deals with desires—whether for love, sex, approval, food or other oral stimulation, such as coffee or cigarettes, and eating disorders. Here also dwell our basic intuitions or *gut feeling*, as it is sometimes called.

The emotional aura layer, like the sacral chakra, rules water within the body—and so issues with fluid retention and hydration, hormones, the reproductive system, the kidneys, fertility, and the bladder. It is a layer especially sensitive to stress.

3. THE MENTAL LAYER: THE THIRD LAYER OF THE AURA

The third layer of the aura is powered by the golden-yellow solar plexus chakra.

This is the layer of the aura that reflects our personal power, confidence, determination, and our unique self. It is often in overdrive in our 24/7, modern, competitive world.

The mental layer and the solar plexus chakra rule digestion, the liver, the spleen, the gallbladder, the abdomen, the stomach, the pancreas, the small intestine, metabolism, the lower back, and the autonomic nervous system.

4. THE ASTRAL LAYER: THE FOURTH LAYER OF THE AURA

The fourth layer of the aura is powered by the rich green heart chakra. Sometimes pink emanates from this aura as well.

This aura level controls the ability to give and receive love, and to understand and empathize with others without drowning in guilt or assuming too much responsibility.

Turquoise, as a slender outer band within this aura strand, is prominent if a person is highly spiritually aware and altruistic.

The astral layer and the heart chakra rule the heart, the chest and breasts, the lungs, the lymph glands, blood pressure and circulation, the upper back, and the skin. It also controls viruses and allergies.

5. THE ETHERIC TEMPLATE: THE FIFTH LAYER OF THE AURA

The fifth layer of the aura is powered by the sky-blue throat chakra.

This is the layer of the aura concerned with creativity, communication, and listening, as well as speaking, formulating and expressing ideas, and developing ideals. Implicated on the autism spectrum, this layer of the aura also controls dreaming.

The etheric template and the throat chakra rule the throat and speech organs, the thyroid gland, the neck and shoulders, the passages that run up to the ears, and the mouth and jaw.

6. THE CELESTIAL BODY: THE SIXTH LAYER OF THE AURA

The sixth layer of the aura is ruled by the indigo brow chakra.

At this aura level, which deals with imagination, inspiration, nightmares, fears, and phobias, your spiritual well-being can affect your physical well-being.

The celestial body and the brow chakra control the eyes, the sinuses, the ears, headaches (including migraines), the pituitary gland, the cerebellum, and the forebrain, and their influence radiates into the central cavity of the brain.

7. THE KETHERIC TEMPLATE OR CAUSAL BODY:

THE SEVENTH LAYER OF THE AURA

The seventh layer of the aura is powered by the crown chakra, whose color is violet, merging into pure white and gold. This is the aura level of total integration of your physical, emotional, psychological, and spiritual self.

The ketheric template and the crown chakra rule the skull, the autoimmune system, all neurological functions, the upper brain, the cerebral cortex, the cerebrum, the central nervous system, hair growth, and the pineal gland. They integrate the functioning of the body, mind, and spirit.

ASSESSING THE WELL-BEING OF THE SEVEN RAINBOW AURA LAYERS USING THE POWER OF TOUCH

This method enables you to feel the seven separate bands using psychometry, or psychic touch, to assess the general condition of your aura, as well as considering any relevant factors in the separate strands. You can also attempt this with friends or family while they are sitting comfortably in a chair.

Trust what your fingers are transmitting through touch but also what you perceive through clairvoyant vision or words in your mind, or even impressions. Eventually, you will begin to sense or even *see* the colors.

Note where in the aura you sense any issues. Can you feel knots or tangles that may be caused by ongoing stress that cannot be openly expressed, say, in the blue etheric template?

Begin in the air directly above your head, about a straight, extended arm span away from your hair. Hold your hands so that your palms face downward. Keeping your hands at an arm's-length distance, slowly move your arms so they are stretched horizontally and your palms face your ears.

Keep them still at about an extended arm span away from your hair. You will sense a slight buzzing, a small electrical charge, and warmth, almost like sparks, where the outer limits of your aura merge into the cosmos.

If you cannot detect anything, move your hands slowly inward, as your aura may be temporarily smaller if you are tired, unwell, or have felt that you are under pressure.

Once located, follow this tingling edge where the aura touches the cosmos around your head and shoulders, still keeping one hand on each side of your head.

Once you have felt the outermost layer, return both hands to the central crown position where you felt the outer limits of the aura and the cosmos. Move both hands, side by side, directly vertically inward through the seventh aura layer to locate by touch a light, almost sticky, sensation that will indicate the inner limits of the seventh aura band and the outermost boundary of the sixth indigo layer of the aura.

When you have located this, move your hands back so that one is on either side of your head, again tracing the aura shape.

Keep moving inward until you have located six layers, each feeling less ethereal as one merges into the other. The innermost edge of the inner aura layer (the red one) will almost touch the hair.

There will be a slight resistance as you move inward through each band. The aura energies emit a rippling sensation—like air blown from a very weak fan—that are most powerfully felt in the outer layers.

Once you have felt the entire aura, move outward again toward the outermost limits, again layer by layer, working very slowly, pausing to feel or sense any lifeless areas, knots or tangles, or jagged lines.

Recording Your Results

When you have finished assessing the health of your aura, draw a head and shoulders in your journal and around it draw seven bands as you did when assessing your mood and personality auras. Mark any problems you found penetrating as many layers as you felt.

Create symbols to indicate each kind of deficiency; for example, zigzag lines for jaggedness, knots for tangles, and empty holes for exhaustion. If the aura is pale all over, you could draw dotted lines across each band. Increased activity could be represented as a series of overlapping spirals.

You will find you know the right colors and shades automatically, but see if any colors are totally missing or overshadowed by an aura color on either side.

CLEANSING AND ENERGIZING THE AURA

Once a week, or when you have had a tiring or challenging few days, use a clear crystal pendulum. The clear pendulum is a conductor of white light energy that is the synthesis of all the colors and, as it moves through the aura, releases whatever colors spontaneously in whatever intensity are needed.

For yourself, work in the aura area around your own head and shoulders; the beneficial results will spread throughout the whole body. When working on others, some people prefer to move the pendulum over the whole aura, head to foot, in front and behind, since the aura surrounds the whole body in an ellipse.

Cleansing the Aura with the Clear Crystal Pendulum

Check your diagram and hold the pendulum so it swings freely, with the chain in your dominant hand.

Swing the pendulum very slowly in counterclockwise spirals in and out of your aura around your head and shoulders, from the outside edges to close in, so it almost brushes your hairline and then out again very slowly as though you were weaving a web of light.

You may feel jaggedness in certain places, like a row of needles sticking outward. At this point the pendulum will spiral fast counterclockwise. You may feel slightly nauseous or your teeth might be set on edge. Jaggedness may penetrate several layers, reflecting a stressful situation.

Trust the pendulum movement and you will know where and how intensely to move the pendulum, still counterclockwise, to untangle a knot, or circle it to smooth particularly harsh colored patches.

If the pendulum suddenly wants to swirl clockwise, allow it to do so. That occurs because the area needs some instant light and energy to overcome some aura resistance. At that point, you may enter a light trance state.

The pendulum will move gently over and over a spot where there is a knot, as if a thread were pulling loose. Tangles, or a group of knots, are reflected by a gradually loosening to-and-fro movement, as if the pendulum were freeing itself.

If the aura is overactive in any band, or maybe two or three, the pendulum will vibrate quite fast and usually swing from side to side. You may feel momentarily irritable or hyped up. Continue to move the pendulum slowly in counterclockwise circles until the feeling eases.

Once you feel a gentle humming buzzing energy, as if a warm heater had been switched on, the pendulum will spontaneously slow down and stop.

Energizing the Aura

Plunge the pendulum nine times into a glass of water, then hold it above a candle or a source of natural light for a few seconds.

Then pass the pendulum in clockwise circles over the whole aura area, again from the outside in and back out rhythmically, recalling where there were faded colors or holes energy had leaked through.

Mend a hole by going over the area repeatedly in small, smooth, clockwise circles, as though you were coloring it in on paper.

You may find the pendulum returning to areas of the aura, as it tunes in to the problem spots that need extra infusions of power.

When the aura is fully energized, the pendulum will slow down.

Finish with three clockwise circles an arm span above the head to seal the energies. For more detailed methods to seal the aura, see Chapter 9 (page 97).

Plunge the pendulum again into the water nine times, and leave it to air-dry.

Checking Your Results

Now recheck the aura with the pendulum and create a new diagram, returning the pendulum to problem areas to cleanse and/or energize.

In the following chapter, I suggest alternative methods for cleansing, healing, and empowering the aura so that you find the best way for yourself.

❖ 6 ❖

STRENGTHENING AND MAINTAINING AURA HEALTH

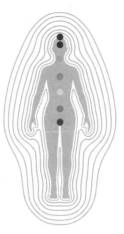

THE ONGOING CARE OF YOUR AURA CAN BECOME PART OF your everyday life, even if you are short of time. You may want to make lasting changes to aura layers over weeks or months. Perhaps you'd like to overcome a negative mood that is always triggered by a specific event or person. Or you might want to modify or bring more to the foreground a particular personality trait. Alternatively, you might want to address a health issue related to one of the bands of the aura.

Regularly working with your aura heals both physical health and emotional issues, and keeps physical as well as emotional problems from recurring so easily in the future.

FILLING YOUR AURA WITH LIGHT, POWER, AND HARMONY

Once a month or before special occasions, such as an interview or a special date, fill your aura with light, radiance, and power from the cosmos so that you spontaneously attract good situations, opportunities, and people. The following technique, practiced regularly, assists in relieving chronic conditions and pain and malaise for which the cause is unknown.

Creating Your Rainbow Charisma Aura

Work in sunlight, moonlight, or by pure white candlelight. Raise your arms and make an arch above your head so your hands curve inward over the center of your head like a cup, but do not let your hands touch your hair (keep them about an arm span from your hair).

Now straighten your arms and point your fingers skyward, both hands close and palms pointing away from you. Either silently or out loud, ask that God/the Goddess, the archangels Gabriel or Raphael (both angels of healing), or your own special guardian angel fill you with light, and that only goodness and healing enter you. You can also ask for any special healing you need.

Picture radiant light, transmitted as pure gold and white rays into your fingertips and down your hands, spiraling through the aura surrounding your body. You may become aware of tingling and golden sparks surrounding your hands.

Keep your hands in position until you can feel your whole aura vibrating with power and radiance.

Now create a cup again with your hands over your head. Working an arm's length away from the top of your head, allow your palms to face inward, with fingers together and curved to move in harmony inward until they reach the sparks sparkling along the outermost edge of the aura above your head, still as white and gold.

Your hands will separate as they move down, still an arm's length away from your body, tracing the outer edge of the aura.

As your hands move slowly down, you will gradually feel the light diffusing into violet, indigo, blue, green, yellow, orange, and red, permeating every layer of the aura right to the red innermost layer just around the body.

When you reach your feet, make another cup with your hands that will synthesize the aura colors once more as white and gold light.

Return your hands to the original arch position above your head by moving them on either side of the body upward until they make the original arch above your head.

The white and gold light from the cup of light at your feet will add shimmers or stars to your aura.

Repeat the whole exercise, from the beginning, six more times but always working from the outermost layer of the aura and allowing the energies to penetrate all seven layers.

Your fingers will be tingling and sparkling. By the time you complete all seven movements, you will feel or see your rainbow getting even brighter and clearer as it encloses you in an ellipse extending in front and behind you. You are enclosed in a rainbow bubble, flowing like warm liquid and spilling beyond you into the cosmos.

Finally, shake your fingers an arm span above your head and the residual white and gold energy sparks will cascade around you, making you feel protected and yet open to new experiences.

When you have finished, plunge your hands into water in which an amethyst and clear crystal quartz have been soaked for eight hours. Dry them on a soft towel.

Thank your guides and angels and then go and wow the world.

THREE VERY FAST WAYS OF KEEPING YOUR AURA BRIGHT AND HEALTHY

Using Water

If you need energy, dip your hands in a bowl of cold water in which you have soaked a clear quartz crystal for eight hours; or, if you are feeling out of balance or restless, use an amethyst.

Sprinkle the water drops over your hair and in the air around the outermost aura edge surrounding your whole body, working an arm span distance all around your head and body.

Keep dipping and sprinkling until you feel refreshed.

Finally, sprinkle some in front of your feet.

To address different needs, see Chapter 7 (page 73) for how you can make crystal waters to strengthen different layers of the aura.

Using Crystals

For a quick aura fix, use a long, pointed, clear quartz crystal or a crystal wand. Hold it pointing outward in your dominant hand and spiral the crystal, starting an arm span out above your head and moving it in and out in alternate clockwise and counterclockwise spirals until you almost brush against the top of your hair. Swing the crystal faster and faster around your head and shoulders, an arm span over your head, for two or three minutes, and then down the left side of your body still at an arm span, moving the crystal in and out of your aura field down in front of your feet and then up the right side to end above the head.

When you cannot move your crystal any faster, repeat the movements, more and more slowly, until you are holding the crystal point up over your head.

Then hold it in, point facing inward, in front of your brow, then your throat, and then your heart, saying,

Above me the light (above head),
Within me the radiance (brow),
That I may be filled (throat),
With love in my heart.

By Checking the lists in chapters 1 and 2, you can find the appropriate crystal and, if you can't get a pointed one, use an elongated tumblestone.

Using Fragrance

Use miniature sage smudge sticks a few inches (several cm) long, or an ordinary lavender, rose, rosemary, sage, or sandalwood incense stick. Choose the appropriate fragrance for any aura level that needs special attention, as specified in Chapters 1 and 2 (page 1 and 15, respectively).

Light the mini-smudge or incense stick and waft the smoke in alternate clockwise and counterclockwise circles an arm span from your body, over your head, and around your feet, until you sense the energies changing.

Work outdoors or in a well-ventilated room. Afterward, leave the source of smoke to burn-through outdoors.

Removing Pollution

If the atmosphere at your home or workplace has been toxic, you can clear pollution from your aura by breathing in light and exhaling darkness. This method will work whether you want to change a mood, if you know a situation brings out a negative aspect of your personality, or if you want to clear part or all of your aura. For example, you might do this if you feel a headache coming on linked to the sixth indigo outer layer of the aura, or you have premenstrual syndrome (governed by the second orange layer), but you must chair a meeting.

Slip away for a minute or two to do this. Or, if you are with people and the atmosphere is tense, you can do it surreptitiously in situ.

Color-breathe while waiting in a supermarket checkout line or at a railway station. This is an excellent and quick way to balancing your aura if you feel fraught or have faced a lot of difficult people or situations.

Breathe in and exhale as you visualize the breath as different colors. This is also an early-morning means of empowering your aura if you slept badly or have a challenging day ahead. You can also end the day in this way, so you relax into a peaceful sleep. Remove general negativity from the aura by exhaling it as dark, dull, or murky colors. Then balance your aura by introducing lighter, brighter hues on the in-breath. For overall aura cleansing and energizing, visualize inhaling white or golden light and exhaling dark or gray light.

WHICH COLOR TO USE

If you have a physical ailment, the lists in Chapter 5 specify which areas of the body or mind need extra attention, so you can send healing or strength to that particular area of the aura. Alternatively, if you feel out of sorts, breathe out the color of the mood aura that is causing the issue and breathe in a softer shade. Or breathe in a brighter shade of the problem color if it is very faded or has holes.

Even more powerfully, since every color has an antidote balancing color, you can use softer shades of the antidote to address an overly harsh aura color and more vibrant shades for holes or faded aura layers. Try both methods and see which works better for you.

If you have a mirror or reflective surface, do an instant assessment of, first, the mood aura, then the personality aura, and finally the seven color bands. With practice, you won't even need to do this; you will *know* which aura band needs fixing.

Beginning Color-Breathing

Take a deep breath through your nose slowly (one . . . and . . . two . . . and . . . three), and hold the breath again for a slow count of three. Exhale slowly through your mouth with a sigh to the same count. If you're out in public, do this subtly.

There are many breathing count patterns, so experiment and use the method with which you are most comfortable.

Do this five or six times.

Visualize the air you are inhaling as pure white or golden light.

Exhale slowly, seeing black mist being expelled, leaving your body lighter and more harmonious.

Slow your breathing a little more, letting golden or white light spread throughout your aura (one . . . and . . . two . . . and . . . three . . . and . . . four), holding your breath and exhaling again (one . . . and . . . two . . . and . . . three . . . and . . . four).

Repeat the pattern, each time visualizing the dark mist leaving your body, becoming paler as the negativity is expelled, until your out-breath feels quite clear. Your aura is now cleansed.

You can adapt this method using the antidote colors below.

Use your exhaled breath, as before, to banish negativity and your inhaled color to introduce calmness or energy, according to your needs. Warmer colors—red, yellow, and orange—are stimulating, and blue, green, and purple—the cooler colors—soothe and gently uplift.

AURA ANTIDOTE COLORS

RED, ETHERIC, FIRST LAYER: Blue

ORANGE, EMOTIONAL, SECOND LAYER: Indigo

YELLOW, MENTAL, THIRD LAYER: Violet

GREEN, ASTRAL, FOURTH LAYER: Orange or blue

BLUE, ETHERIC TEMPLATE, FIFTH LAYER: Red

INDIGO, CELESTIAL BODY, SIXTH LAYER: Orange

VIOLET, KETHERIC TEMPLATE, SEVENTH LAYER: Yellow

Antidotes for Other Colors in the Aura

BLACK: White

BROWN: Yellow or blue

GOLD: Silver

GRAY: White

MAGENTA: Bright blue

PINK: Rich sky-blue or darker blue

SILVER: Gold

TURQUOISE: Soft green or blue

WHITE: Silver or a contrasting shade of white; milky for increased harshness; bright white for pale

CREATING ANTIDOTE REMEDIES

Antidote colors, like softer or brighter shades of a problem aura color, can be added in crystals, flowers, or food, by lighting candles, by wearing appropriately colored clothing, or by visualizing the needed counterbalancing color or shade.

If a suitable color is not available, a white candle can be lit. Picture the color you need coming out from the candle as a ray of light.

Using Antidote Crystals

Worn as jewelry, crystals can address a chronic condition associated with an aura level or modify a recurring mood or an undesirable personality trait. Crystals of an appropriate shade can be carried (use one for each aura layer if the whole aura is unbalanced), left in dishes around the home or workplace, and soaked in water. That water can then be drunk, be used in baths, or be splashed on your aura when you feel stressed.

Alternatively, breathe in the antidote color by holding the crystal in open cupped hands near your mouth as you gently inhale and exhale, absorbing the powers of the crystal.

The crystals for each aura layer are listed in Chapters 1 and 2 (page 1 and 15, respectively). See Chapter 7 (page 73) for how to make aura crystal waters.

Using Fragrances

Fragrant herbs and flowers, whether used as incense, as oils in a burner or diffuser, as fragrant candles, or, better still, as candles in their natural form, contain pure life force to heal and strengthen different layers of the aura. Breathe in the aura colors associated within the fragrance (pages 4-13) and you breathe in their strengths. A fragrant garden in sunlight or moonlight is a great aura restorative. Or use herb pots in your kitchen.

Add oils or scented products in your bath or as fragrance or oils dabbed on pulse points. Mix two or three in a burner or burn different scented candles to work with more than one layer.

In the next chapter, we will work with the collective auras of the home and workplace, and interpret what is going on between people in a workplace or at a social gathering through their aura interactions.

AURAS IN THE HOME AND WORKPLACE

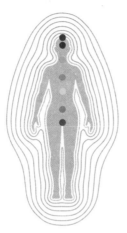

AURAS REVEAL HIDDEN INFORMATION AS WE INTERACT with neighbors, friends, family members, and colleagues—in the workplace and at any social gathering. By studying these aura connections, you can almost instantly grasp the dynamics of any situation, avoiding the pitfalls and seeing possibilities for creating positive links, even with difficult people.

HOW TO STUDY AURA INTERACTIONS

The auras of individual family members, and people in the workplace or at social gatherings, are constantly interacting, whether positively or negatively. They may try to dominate and manipulate (watch out for murky yellows and greens), or they may merge, like a constantly flowing sea, to create a harmonious, collective aura in the home or workplace.

It's easy to read aura interactions. Lines can come from anywhere in the sender's aura but are usually perceived emanating from around the sender's brow, between and just above eyes. They are received in the same place.

TUNING IN TO AURA INTERACTIONS

Relax, half-closing your eyes, allowing your eyes to go into soft focus as you people-watch in a connected group, whether extended family, an office setting, a seminar, or a larger gathering, such as a wedding or a graduation.

Look for interconnecting lines and shades of color moving between people, noting people who have no lines connecting with them, or who send out a lot of them but don't receive connections back. Also watch for people who receive a lot of attention but don't respond emotionally. Even within the lines, be aware of dark knots or overly harsh shades.

Love aura rays are always strong, but are they a possessive pea green or pale green, indicating unrequited love, or is there a two-way, rich, green energy?

WORKING WITH AURAS IN FAMILY, WORKPLACE, AND SOCIAL INTERACTIONS

Connecting rays are usually mood aura links. However, the mood aura may be influenced by the underlying personality aura in terms of suppressed personality clashes or strong compatibilities. Intense compatibility happens in love, where, if lovers are standing close to each other, both their auras may seem to merge.

If family and social gatherings or workplace meetings cause conflict, plotting aura interactions can help you understand the underlying dynamics, avoid pitfalls, and find out who is generating the difficulty. The person you thought was a sweet old aunt, the office mouse, or a long-standing gym member furiously pumping iron in the corner might actually be the ones slyly stirring the pot.

Study group auras everywhere—nights out with friends, a family dinner at home, a major wedding, when meeting new family members, when you're starting a new job, or wherever new people gather. What people say and even their body language, which can be controlled, do not necessarily reflect what is going on inside.

Write notes on your phone in situ to remind yourself of what you perceive. At a party, scribble your observations on the back of a napkin.

Afterward, on a large piece of paper, plot the group dynamics at the celebration or other gathering. Draw and name circles representing each character you observed closely, and use colored pencils or very fine marker brushes in a variety of shades to draw the interconnecting rays and plot the connections.

Draw the rays going *to* each of the people from an individual as a single line and those coming back toward them as a separate line, with arrows on each to indicate the direction the rays are traveling.

For rays falling short of the intended recipient, place a vertical line at the end.

Once you have drawn the rays between everybody, your figure will resemble a spiderweb. Who has the most rays going toward them? Who is sending out the most, trying to be the life and soul of the party? Are the people in the family or social gathering communicating and, if so, are they expressing themselves in positive ways and with positive intent? Note the shades and you'll discover if anyone is totally isolated by choice, sending out repelling rays.

Notice auras with hooked lines, like tentacles, which are manipulative or possessive. Conversely, observe sociable rays, reaching out like rays of the sun everywhere. Some rays may be closed and compact or misty and secretive, even though the person may appear outgoing in their words and actions.

Follow the line to where it ends, or the person nearest to where it ends, if it stops short and disperses.

REMEDIAL ACTIONS TO CREATE HAPPY GATHERINGS

If the people and situation, such as a workplace, are familiar to you, you will see patterns emerging and can prepare in advance to deflect negative rays and amplify positive ones. You may notice, in time, that a mist or fog or bright sunshine, at home or in the workplace, generates a collective aura hanging over all the individuals present. Such a collective aura can linger, even when the people contributing to it are not present. Over time, it may generate a good or bad overall atmosphere and create negative aura connections, even between normally peace-loving folk. Following are remedial actions you can take to create happy gatherings at home, in relationships, at work, and at social functions.

These actions can be adapted to the workplace if certain individuals at a daily meeting seem to generate negativity even before they speak or the atmosphere is instantly unwelcoming or overly harsh and competitive. A collective aura in any buildings that are regularly used, such as a gym, an office, homes, and social clubs, can build up over months and years. So look up and see if the place has an independent aura that needs modifying, especially if people are constantly quarreling or regularly taking time off work due to stress.

Using Crystals

Crystals are the easiest and most effective means of bringing about aura harmony. Keep dishes of mixed-color crystals in living areas or workspaces to deflect problems or keep a bag or purse of them to carry to areas in the workplace where collective negative energies abound or areas clashing people frequent. Add crystal waters to drinks at home, at social gatherings, at your workplace, or in a bowl in which flowers are floated.

You can use:

- Softly hued crystals—blue lace agate, amethyst, blue and pink chalcedony, jade, mangano or pink calcite, any fluorites, opals, and moonstones—to encourage gentle loving interactions at home or to mute an overly harsh, dominant individual aura or an overly competitive workplace aura.

- Vibrant crystals—brown tigereye, amber, carnelian, clear quartz, sparkling yellow citrine, garnet, and herkimer diamond—to counter lethargic interactions or lack of communication and to revive enthusiasm.

- Strong crystals—blue lapis lazuli, sodalite, purple sugilite, and green and black malachite—to calm panic and anxiety and bring about honest, open communication.

- Cloudy, dark crystals—smoky quartz, Apache tear, rutilated quartz, obsidian, and polished flint—to absorb angry or confrontational vibes or spite and sarcasm.

Using Fragrances

Fragrant growing plants and herbs form a psychic aura shield and soothe irritability and hyperactivity.

- Add herbs to recipes or freshly chopped herbs to a salad bowl. Check Chapters 1 and 2 for color associations.

- Use mint and rosemary to counter spite, sage to soothe anger and irritability, basil to promote well-being, chamomile to encourage kindness, and ginger to generate enthusiasm and optimism.

Using Color Sources

You can try:

- Soft blue, pink, or green candles, lit at dinner or around a room where the family or friends will relax for warm connections, to ease frequent temper tantrums, rigid attitudes, or angst.

- Fresh oranges, golden peaches, green apples, yellow bananas, red plums, blueberries, black and red currants, and grapes (purple, red, or green) in dishes around a room for freshening tired auras and diminishing lingering resentments. People will invariably choose the fruit whose color their aura most needs for balance.

- Brown nuts and seeds to ease panic and slow down overdrive.

Making Crystal Waters

For fast effect, make crystal elixirs or waters. Then, add the liquid to tea, coffee, or juice, or consume it as drinking water (only a drop or two is needed) as an antidote to dominant individuals or a negative collective mood aura.

Choose crystals in the right shade and color. For an overly harsh color, use a softer shade of the antidote crystal, and for a faded one use a brighter shade.

Use crystal elixirs to strengthen or heal your own aura as well.

Put the crystal(s) into a jug or a wide-necked glass bottle and fill the jug or bottle two-thirds full with water.

According to the amount of water you require, add an appropriate number of crystals, one to 250 ml (a quarter of a pint), two or double-size for 500 ml, and so on.

Add two or more different-colored crystals if there are different auras to be modified. An aura will only take in the colors it needs, no matter how many are used.

For energizing water, select clear quartz. For calming water, amethyst or rose quartz is best. Use rose quartz water for love, and jade to restore health to a tired aura and to encourage the faithful green of love to shine more brightly, if dimmed.

Leave energizing crystals in daylight for an hour or so. Softer shades should be exposed after dark or in moonlight.

If a crystal is porous or toxic in water, such as metallic ones like pyrites or green malachite (if you're uncertain of a crystal's toxicity, check in a crystal or mineral book, such as my *Complete Crystal Handbook*), float the crystals in a small sealed jar in a bowl of water for a few hours and use the water in which you floated the crystals.

ABSORBING COLOR DIRECTLY

Breathing out color is the most immediate and powerful way of diffusing antidote colors to people and situations.

Use natural sources of color whenever possible, held in your cupped hands, or touch a flower or a piece of fruit.

However, you can absorb necessary aura energies to breathe out from any color source—marker pens taken to a workplace meeting, a picture on the wall, a lighted candle, different-colored fabrics as clothes or throws, painted wooden objects or ceramics, even children's toys or the blue sky viewed from a window.

If an immediate color source doesn't present itself, visualize a large sphere of the appropriate color in front of you.

Look directly toward the person who needs the color aura boost, or upward for a collective negative shade change, breathe in the color through your nose and exhale it as a soft or silent sigh in the direction of the person about to launch an attack.

Release in your imagination arrowlike rays of colored light from your third eye area in the center of your brow as straight parallel lines toward the aura of the person who needs it or upward to modify a collective aura.

Gradually, you will feel the color flow from you, spontaneously slowing and stopping.

AURAS IN THE WORKPLACE

Workplace auras offer a good guide to understanding your workplace— who holds the reins of power, what unspoken alliances have been forged, and how, if you are new, you can best merge into the culture and eventually make your mark. If yours is a managerial role, studying aura interconnections can help you to decide the best combinations of workers in a team and to identify hidden challenges to your authority.

Exactly as you did in social situations, begin by plotting the interactions and connections between the auras of people you work with on a typical day.

Make observations on different days if certain people are absent; one or two strong personalities can alter the whole balance of power and harmony.

Plot the auras to work out the source and nature of the antipathy, or perhaps strong attraction, between two unlikely people. Is there an emotionally needy person who is trying to send out tentacles to everyone? The aura readings of two or three significant characters may change your perception of the victim/villain roles and explain mutual dependencies or personal power games.

Observe any significant mood changes that occur during the day. During an argument or when someone is the object of criticism, one aura may become significantly paler or less vibrant. The openly weaker of the two or three may be a disguised psychological bully and may be making the other person feel guilty (watch out for murky greens around an emotional vampire).

Occasionally, the victim may be drawing power from the tyrant and is unconsciously colluding in the scenario. Who is controlling the interaction?

You can use the same ways of modifying the collective aura of the workplace or troublesome individuals at work as you did for the home and in social situations.

AURA MIRRORING

It is possible for one person to deliberately mirror another person's aura or the overall aura energy above an interviewing panel or work-place group. This is a useful tactic to adopt in social settings or in the workplace.

As the auras blend, the other person or group relaxes as they increasingly feel that you are like them. They will react more positively to your suggestions and, indeed, your very presence.

Look toward the person whose aura you wish to mirror or a representative member of an interviewing panel or official board.

Focus on what seems like the predominant aura color(s) of the mood or the facet of the personality being projected. It might be a logical, cool yellow; a rich, powerful blue (in this case make yours slightly paler so as not to present a challenge); or a deep green, good for the sympathy vote.

Now you are going to draw her predominant aura color temporarily over yours.

As you look toward the target person, *feel* how much you like her and sympathize with her viewpoint.

Slowly draw in your mind's eye, from the target rays of her aura color, with your lips slightly apart on each in-breath, and breathe out any dislike or doubts as pale mist.

Persevere until you *feel* your aura color change to mirror that of the chosen target.

In the next chapter, we will look at the aura of pets and how we can improve their well-being by healing their auras.

❖ 8 ❖

THE AURAS OF PETS

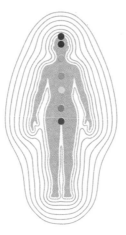

PETS, LIKE PEOPLE, HAVE DISTINCTIVE AURAS. **R**EADING AND
understanding your pet's aura help you anticipate the
moods and needs of an animal and minimize behavior
problems.

Aura information also helps you choose the right pet from a
litter or rescue center.

IDENTIFYING ANIMAL AURA LAYERS

The auras of mammals and companion animals differ from those
of humans, consisting of three or four layers in a horizontal ellipse
around the body. These aura layers progress outward, the innermost
species layer brushing against fur or feathers.

An animal's three main aura layers—species, mood, and personality aura—link with that animal's three most active chakras—the

root, sacral, and solar plexus, respectively—the three innermost layers in humans.

In addition, every creature has small sensory chakras that absorb information, in each paw or claw, on the tips of the ears, around the nose, over each eye, and on the wings and tail feathers of birds, and energize the species aura as fight or flight.

Fish, reptiles, and insects have a single aura layer.

OBSERVING ANIMAL AURAS

In wild and companion animals, the innermost band closely follows the contours of the body and the other two layers become less defined farther from the fur or feathers. When the pet is moving, angry, or excited, the aura flares in all directions, especially from the mood layer that temporarily overwhelms the others. If a creature is trying to dominate his owner or other pets, the personality aura may cover the other layers.

In healthy, happy creatures the personality layer meets the cosmos, the whole aura extending about the same distance away from the body in all directions as the length from the front leg to the paw or claw and, in creatures with long legs, about a third to half that distance. You can feel it in the same ways as touching the human aura (see Chapter 3, page 27).

To *see* all layers of the aura, wait until the animal is relaxed, half-close your eyes, and let your eyes go into soft focus as you did to observe the seven bands of the human aura.

THE SPECIES AURA BAND

The species color is common to creatures of the same species.

The species band is strongest around the paws or claws, the back, and the genitals, and is rippled. It may seem to be joined to the fur or feathers.

The root chakra directly empowers the species aura.

The species aura is related to physical needs and basic reproductive urges, as well as territorial instincts. This aura is strongest in wild animals with little contact with humans and weakest in urban pets that spend most of their time indoors or are pampered.

The Mood Aura

This forms the middle, most volatile layer, constantly moving with flashes and sparkles. It corresponds with the sacral chakra. The mood aura offers a key to the creature's feelings and needs, and is an early warning system if an animal is jealous of a newcomer or spoiling for a fight.

The Personality Aura

The personality band, which forms the outermost layer of the aura, remains relatively consistent through the creature's life.

If an animal has been traumatized by bad treatment or abandonment, dark cloudy waves obscure the natural personality aura.

The personality aura is ruled by the solar plexus chakra and determines how strong a character a pet has and its idiosyncrasies.

The personality color is strong around the upper stomach and shoulders, with a smooth matte texture, most clearly observed when the pet is relaxed or asleep.

The Soul Aura

Intelligent creatures with strong telepathic links with owners or who work as helper dogs to the disabled, or rescue animals, have an additional aura layer. This corresponds to the heart chakra and is most visible around the heart, head, and shoulders. Colors may be turquoise or purple, and manifest as an ethereal layer beyond the personality aura.

THE AURA COLORS IN AN ANIMAL
Red

SPECIES AURA: Red is not a pet aura, except in an adopted cat that had been living wild, a litter of feral strays, or a stallion bred from wild stock. Red is seen around sharks and killer whales, all predatory animals, especially jungle cats, bulls, rams, and birds of prey.

MOOD AURA: Bright red is a sign of good health and shows a need for exercise or stimulating activity, good before an animal competes. If this aura is harsh or metallic red, your pet is feeling aggressive and may attack another animal or person, even if he's normally docile. A flashing scarlet aura shows a creature that is ready to mate.

PERSONALITY AURA: A red personality aura shows fearlessness and readiness for action. A harsh red aura indicates innate aggression and a dull red aura indicates irritability or snappishness. Even if small, the creature with a red personality aura will be very territorial and ready to attack even larger creatures.

Orange

SPECIES AURA: Independent species that live apart from humans and do not rely on them except to forage tend to have orange species auras. These include stags, hares, foxes, wild boar, and wild cats, as well as faithful creatures whose mates have died, such as swans, horses, and gibbons.

MOOD AURA: A clear orange aura is confident but doesn't like to be petted. It's a common color among cats, and those with an orange mood aura can be possessive about toys and their sleeping areas. A dark orange aura appears in animals teased by small children. A pale orange aura indicates an animal bullied by other pets. A brilliant orange signals that your pet is in a mood to escape.

PERSONALITY AURA: An orange personality aura characterizes pets of any species that are by nature loners and give love to their owner on their own terms. They can't be bribed, they're happy in their own company, and they do not mind being left alone while you're at work.

Yellow

SPECIES AURA: Intelligent animals who communicate directly with humans—dogs, horses, cats, budgerigars, and parrots—generally have a yellow aura. Also included among them are creatures that live in family groups, such as gorillas, orangutans, and chimpanzees.

MOOD AURA: A clear yellow mood aura shows that it's a good time to train an animal, especially verbally. Dirty mustard yellow indicates jealousy, if a new human or pet has entered the home.

PERSONALITY AURA: A creature with a yellow personality aura is easily trained but easily bored, good company if you live alone. These creatures prefer adults to children.

Green

SPECIES AURA: Animals of any domesticated species that are naturally faithful and loving to owners may have a green species aura. These include flock and herd animals, and aquatic creatures.

MOOD AURA: A green mood aura reflects relatively stable, loving pet-owner relationships, which deepen during grooming or petting and become pale if you are feeling sad, as the animal is tuned in to your emotions.

PERSONALITY AURA: Bright green indicates a pet that loves you unconditionally, but does not like being left alone too long. A pale green aura signals that a pet is pining for an absent family member or animal. Muddy green shows that the animal is possessive toward her owner.

Blue

SPECIES AURA: A blue species aura is not often seen around domestic pets. It mainly characterizes wise species, such as elephants, dolphins, and whales, as well as storks, cranes, flamingos, herons, and other tall, graceful birds. The species aura of eagles and hawks may also be tinged with gold, while streaks of silvery blue may appear around flocks of birds in flight and shoals of marine fish.

MOOD AURA: When the animal's aura is clear or sky-blue, your pet will anticipate your unspoken thoughts but won't be in the mood for roughhousing. Dark blue says it's not a time for changes in routine, being taken to the vet, or going on a major outing.

PERSONALITY AURA: Sky-blue or turquoise auras in any creature mark a wise soul, tuned in to the needs of humans and able to perform complex tasks for disabled owners. This may appear in the soul aura. The pet with a blue personality aura needs to be the alpha or only pet in a home. A dark blue aura shows love of routine and being well-groomed.

Purple (incorporates indigo and violet)

SPECIES AURA: A purple species aura characterizes very aristocratic-natured cats and horses (not necessarily those with pedigrees), butterflies, small monkeys (such as marmosets and tamarinds), chinchillas, and exotic birds (such as canaries, parakeets, birds of paradise, and sunbirds).

MOOD AURA: If an animal's mood aura suddenly turns bright purple and the animal seems to be looking intently at something you cannot see, he may be picking up the friendly presence of a former pet or a deceased loving relative. Pale purple indicates that your altruistic pet may need tender loving care and a rest.

PERSONALITY AURA: Clairvoyant and mystical, any pet with a purple personality aura has strong telepathic links with you and will have chosen *you*. When your pet's aura turns pale purple, she may have decided to move on. This is another color that may appear in the soul aura. If your purple-aura pet doesn't like a stranger, beware.

Pink

SPECIES AURA: The females of all species display soft pink auras when they are pregnant, giving birth, or caring for their young. Rabbits, guinea pigs, and other small animals kept as pets also tend to permanently display this aura, especially females.

MOOD AURA: Like green, a clear pink mood aura is often seen in a well-loved pet, especially in family situations. The color will increase when you feel lonely and unloved, as your pet sends you waves of love.

PERSONALITY AURA: A clear pink personality aura confirms, in males and females alike, patience and gentleness with small children and other animals. A pet with this personality aura will care for abandoned ones. This would be an ideal animal companion for a sick person or someone who lives alone. A pet with a pale pink aura may be clingy and overanxious.

Brown

SPECIES AURA: Brown should be present in the species aura of all animal pets, even city ones; its absence can reveal that animals are losing touch with their natural instincts and becoming overly domesticated. Golden brown appears in creatures that spend hours outdoors, working animals, donkeys, countryside cats, and free-range pigs and poultry. This species aura is seen among pack animals, such as wolves, around bears, in wild rabbit colonies, and around hive bees and garden birds. Sandy brown is observed around lizards, snakes, and reptiles.

MOOD AURA: A clear or rich brown mood aura, a sign of contentment, is most often seen when a pet is outdoors having fun. Pale brown indicates that the creature needs more contact with nature. A dull, brown aura in an elderly animal means that the creature needs peace and quiet.

PERSONALITY AURA: A clear shade of brown indicates good protectors. The pet likes living with a larger human family, including children, and with other animals of its own kind. The pet also enjoys any home where the family or owner spends a lot of time outdoors.

Gray

SPECIES AURA: Gray is associated with shy pets; hamsters, gerbils, rodents, chipmunks, turtles, and tortoises; all nocturnal or burrowing creatures, such as badgers, hedgehogs, and moles; and moths and most other insects.

MOOD AURA: A gray mood aura reflects a temporarily anxious or confused creature. A misty aura may indicate that your animal has another home or food supply.

PERSONALITY AURA: Whatever the species, your gray creature will be happiest and liveliest in the evenings, constantly finding hiding places and storing food. Those with a gray personality aura are not generally suitable as companion animals.

Black

PERSONALITY/MOOD AURA: This is seen around old, sick creatures gradually letting go of life, as well as in animals that have been abandoned or cruelly treated. If an animal displays a harsh metallic or black jagged aura, he is best left to a sanctuary or adopted by one owner who can lavish on him great care.

USING CRYSTALS TO MAINTAIN THE HEALTH OF YOUR PET'S AURA

With pets, treating the whole aura is often easiest and most effective, since they are all closely interconnected. However, you can use antidote crystals in ways suggested below for specific aura color issues, substituting them for the general crystals specified below.

For maintaining a pet's aura health and for improving a dull aura, set four moss or tree agates or small jade crystals under a pet bed, in the corners of a stable, or wherever the animal regularly sleeps.

Give your animal or bird water to drink in which a jade crystal or, in the case of a very stressed animal, an amethyst crystal has been soaked overnight.

Once a week, when your pet is resting or asleep, strengthen her aura field and remove excesses of harsh energy by circling clockwise a few inches (several cm) over her a sparkling yellow citrine or a clear quartz crystal, held in your dominant hand and a soft pink rose quartz or any calcite in the other hand, counterclockwise.

Move the crystals around the whole aura area, spiraling in and out so it brushes against her fur and then out to approximately the same distance as halfway down the front leg to the paw or claw. In creatures with long legs, the distance should be about a quarter to a third of this length.

Send color-breathing energies to any pets whose auras are pale or who are flickering, revealing anxiety, by holding a crystal or crystals in the appropriate color in your open cupped hand, breathing in the color, and gently exhaling it toward the animal.

An Alternative Way to Cleanse and Heal Your Pet's Aura

Begin by stroking your pet on the back and the head very slowly with the fingertips of your dominant hand.

Move your hand an inch or two (several cm) above the fur or skin and, using both hands, continue to stroke the pet with gentle rhythmic movements, so that you are not touching his fur, but rather the air around him, following the contours of his body.

Move your hands progressively farther away inch by inch (cm by cm), still following the approximate line of his body, until you feel that the connection has ceased. This is the outer edge of the aura.

Keep moving your fingers gently from the outermost limits of the aura in toward the fur and out again.

Your hands will spontaneously take longer on certain areas or return to specific spots. You may sense an untangling if there is a knot.

Your hands will slow spontaneously when the cleansing is completed, usually between five and fifteen minutes.

In the final chapter, we will work with sealing and protecting your aura and that of your pets, so you and they are fully alert but guarded against negative influences.

❖ 9 ❖

SEALING AND PROTECTING THE AURA IN DAILY LIFE

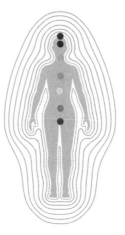

SEALING YOUR AURA AFTER CLEANSING AND EMPOWERING IT allows positive energies to enter your aura and filters out negativity and undue stress from daily life. Over time, negativity and stress can undermine your health and well-being.

SEALING THE AURA WITH LIGHT

Sit or stand with your hands about 2–3 inches (5–8 cm) apart, palms vertical and facing each other.

Move your palms together so they almost touch, then move them slowly outwards 2–3 inches (5–8 cm) again, keeping them vertical all the time.

Repeat this gradual in-and-out movement of your palms, progressively decreasing the distance between the palms as you move them outward and go in again.

Your hands will become heavier, feel attracted like magnets, and be quite sticky as the aura energies of both hands merge.

You may notice a silvery white shimmer around each hand as it becomes progressively harder to separate them.

When your palms are no more than ¾ of an inch (2 cm) apart, lift your hands and arms over the center of your head to where you feel the outer limits of the aura. This outer edge of the newly cleansed and energized aura will be so sparkly and vibrating that it will be hard to miss.

Form a cup shape over your head with your hands, palms facing down and fingers together, around the outer aura edge.

Slowly follow the contours of the outer edge, letting each hand spontaneously move in unison down the sides of your body. You may encounter pressure, as though the outline of the aura is solidifying.

Stoop naturally, as though drawing an ellipse shape down each side of your body, still following the outermost aura limit with an invisible crayon, and end in front of your feet.

Finally, shake your fingers all around your head and shoulders, keeping the same arm span distance, and you will see or sense silver sparks or stars outlining the aura.

Soft silver light will flow into the aura, all around your body— front, back, and from head to toe.

Finally, run your hands an extended arm span away down both sides of your body and then down the front, as though you were brushing off any excess aura energies with a hairbrush.

Bring these unseen aura energies down to the ground.

Then, briefly, hold your hands over a candle (not too close!) or in sunlight to cleanse them. You can do aura brushing any time during the day if someone has made you feel uncomfortable by getting too close to your aura space.

Either brush the unwanted aura energy to the ground, or roll it into an imaginary ball and drop it out of a window or even into a trash can. This is a way of symbolically removing unwanted energies from your space.

Seal the Aura of Your Pet

After healing, cleansing, or empowering your pet's aura, stand, sit, or kneel so you are facing your pet.

Hold your hands for a minute or two over a green plant or yellow flowers in a pot, palms inward and fingers together, until you feel your fingers tingling.

Now move your hands, palms facing inward, toward each other and out again, an inch or two (2–5 cm) away, moving each hand closer to the other, until you feel the power building up, this time picturing the rich green and golden-brown light of nature flowing in and around your fingertips.

When your hands are almost touching, hold them straight out in front of you, fingers directed toward your pet.

Picture green and gold light flowing from your hands into your pet's body and spilling out into the energy field through all three or four layers, to seal and protect your pet's aura with love.

A GOLDEN AURA SHIELD FOR PHYSICAL, EMOTIONAL, AND SPIRITUAL PROTECTION

Usually aura sealing keeps your aura safe. However, if you are under a lot of external stress or you feel you are under psychic or psychological attack, a "shield of gold" will repel all harm, from whatever source or of whatever kind, and leave you feeling confident and able to handle anything.

Once created, the aura or energy shield can be activated instantly in any setting or circumstance.

Sometimes you'll encounter a person who is overwhelmingly negative or so consumed by her own ingrained beliefs that you would be banging your head against a solid aura wall if you tried to modify her mood or entrenched personality. In this case, you may need to protect your own aura.

CREATING YOUR PSYCHIC ENERGY SHIELD OF GOLD

You only need to renew your shield's strength every three months or so, unless you have been under heavy attack. In that case, re-create it every week or month until the danger or nastiness passes.

Creating a Golden Aura Shield for Protection

The solar plexus, located around the center of the upper stomach where the rib cage ends, empowers the third mental layer of the aura. This is the vital source of power for the golden shield and your inner sun and can protect you from all harm.

Move your hand with your palm innermost around the center of your upper stomach and you will gradually experience a sensation like holding your hand over an emptying bath.

Remove your hand when you feel it tingling.

Now connect physically with the color gold. Hold a gold earring or ring, or stare at a gold color source, such as a gold-colored dish filled with golden fruit, a golden crystal like chalcopyrite or amber, a piece of gold foil, or a lit gold candle.

Close your eyes and picture the gold flooding your inner vision and entering your body through every pore.

Keep your eyes open, staring at the gold, then close them until you can *see* nothing but gold in your mind and *feel* warm liquid gold entering your body.

Now, with eyes open to connect with the source of gold, picture golden light flowing downward into your body, through the crown of your head. This is often called the "Archangel Michael light."

Simultaneously, visualize rich golden streams rising up through your feet from Mother Earth, the source of physical gold, swirling in your solar plexus, illuminating your inner sun.

Sit, observing your external source of gold and letting golden light flow within you and around your aura.

When you feel yourself glowing inside, say three times, *I am pure gold*.

Now we are going to use this inner body of gold to create a defensive shield around your aura, radiating out into the cosmos.

Sit holding the fingers and palms of your hands vertically facing and almost touching each other. Then move them apart quickly.

You have done this before, but now you will move on to the next stage in manipulating aura energies. Continue to move your hands together and apart more and more slowly together and apart, but not quite touching, until this time you can *see* and *feel* the golden energy as a ball of light with golden sparks building up around your hands.

Form an energy ball from this invisible, sticky, golden substance between your hands, as if you were rolling between your hands a ball of very sticky clay, making it any size, from a tennis ball to a small football.

When you can fully feel its roundness and firmness, rest the invisible ball against your solar plexus and you will start to *see* and/or *feel* the inner gold from your inner sun filling the ball.

With your eyes closed, psychically rotate the invisible ball in your hands until you sense that the ball is complete and glowing golden.

Creating the Golden Shield

Still holding the energy ball, sit with your knees together, raise your arms above your head in an arch, lifting the energy ball so it is an arm span above your head.

Dig your fingers into the aura energies within your golden ball until it bursts open and the golden substance cascades like a waterfall down your sides, in front of you and behind, completely enclosing you and surrounding you about the distance of an extended arm span, clear enough so you can see right through it. You will feel as if you're being bathed in golden warm shimmering water.

Gradually, *see* and/or *feel* the shell of the protective sphere hardening into an iridescent gold, mingling with a mother-of-pearl edge so that only loving thoughts from others may enter and any negative feelings from whatever source will be repelled.

Now clap above your head to complete the seal.

Allow the golden shield around your aura to fade, but know it is there in the background, waiting to be activated.

Activating Your Shield of Gold When You Are Under Threat

Whenever you need your shield of gold, say in your mind I call my shield of gold to guard me from all harm and, if you wish, ask Archangel Michael to strengthen your shield from fierce attack.

Withdrawing Your Aura

You may wish to withdraw your aura when you wish to maintain a low profile to avoid confrontation or potential hazards. For example, if someone is tired or ill, his naturally contracted aura is no more than an inch or two (several cm) from the skin. With practice, it is possible, for short periods, to withdraw the aura so that it is entirely within the physical body. This is a good technique whenever you wish or need to remain unnoticed.

Deliberately quiet your thoughts so that your aura is not fueled by anxiety or fear, somewhat like putting a car in neutral.

If you are in a dark place, breathe in the gentle blackness though your nose and, as you inhale, contract and tense your muscles, feeling the aura move closer to your skin.

Breathe out doubts and fears as harsh red light and relax your muscles.

Keep doing this and, bit by bit, your aura will contract. Continue until you feel a gentle tug as your aura is pulled level with your skin, like an umbrella folding up or a tent being pushed back into its bag.

Breathe gently, slowly, and deeply until danger or fear has passed.

When it is safe, stretch your body and shake your fingers to reactivate the normal aura field.

Creating an Aura of Grayness

An alternative is to cover your aura with misty grayness, when you are in a vulnerable position or would like to be undisturbed. The grayness masks the normal auric signals we emit when we are afraid or anxious.

Though you can create this aura shield in advance, you may wish to repeat the steps of the whole process in your mind in situ when you are feeling under threat, as it is very calming.

Work in the evening, as it gets dark, or on a misty, dull day, and light a gray candle.

Sit in a comfortable position and close your eyes. Use your inner psychic screen to picture the candle flame as if your eyes were open and you were looking at it directly.

Breathe slowly and evenly, deep into your rib cage, and sigh out any feelings of panic, doubt, or any specific fears.

On the inner screen, imagine the swirling seven aura colors around your head and body entering the candle flame and flowing out as gray mist, so you can hardly see the candle. This time the shield effect will be like gray mist, rather than a sealed sphere like the golden shield.

When you can no longer see the candle flame in the mist, open your eyes and blow out the actual candle flame. You may or may not physically see the mist effect around the actual candle, but this does not matter.

Light one or two white candles to restore light to your aura.

Whenever you feel under threat, say in your mind or out loud if you are alone, *I wear the cloak of invisibility and so I pass unseen.*

You can re-create this aura of gray monthly or whenever needed.

When the danger has passed, picture the mist dispersing and your aura once more unfolding and growing bright.

A RAINBOW RITUAL

Here is a ritual to synthesize all your aura energies and fill your aura with color and light. Take seven small candles—red, orange, yellow, green, blue, indigo, and violet—and place them in a circle in that order.

Sit facing the candles.

Light the red candle, saying, *Red for strength and courage and so my aura is filled with joy and harmony.*

Light the orange candle, saying, *Orange for confidence and so my aura is filled with joy and harmony.*

Light the yellow candle, saying, *Yellow for power and so my aura is filled with joy and harmony.*

Light the green candle, saying, *Green for love and so my aura is filled with joy and harmony.*

Light the blue candle, saying, *Blue for abundance and so my aura is filled with joy and harmony.*

Light the indigo candle, saying, *Indigo for wisdom and so my aura is filled with joy and harmony.*

Light the violet candle, saying, *Violet brings synthesis and so my aura is filled with joy and harmony.*

When you are ready, blow out each candle in reverse order of lighting, saying for each, *Now my aura is filled with the joy of the rainbow.*

ABOUT THE AUTHOR

Cassandra Eason is an international author and broadcaster on all aspects of crystals, folklore, Celtic wisdom, Wicca, sacred sites, earth energies, divinations, and natural magic. She has studied aura interactions for over twenty-five years, written several books and courses on auras, and has taught people internationally to interpret and heal their auras. She uses aura reading as part of her regular consultations with clients. Cassandra has published over eighty books on different aspects of healing, magick, divination, and energy work, including *The Complete Crystal Handbook* and *A Spell a Day.*

INDEX

Note: page numbers in parentheses indicate non-contiguous references in sequential pages.

A

Anael, 8
Archangels, color associations, (5–8), (10–13), 16, 17, (19–23), 25
Ariel, 21
Astral layer, 53

B

Breathing
  color-breathing, 68–69, 70–71, 80–81, 83, 95
  creating aura of grayness, 104–105
  out doubts and fears, 104
  removing pollution, 66–67

C

Camael, 5
Cassiel, 11, 22, 25
Causal body, 54
Celestial body, 53–54
Chakras
  brow or third eye, 4, 11, 18, 53–54, 65, 81
  color correspondences, (4–6), (8–13)
  crown/predominant, 4, 12, 13, 18, 43, 54, 101
  heart, 4, 9, 19, 20, 21, 44, 53, 88
  illustrated, 4
  root or base, 4, 5, 22, 24, 25, 50, 51, 86, 87
  sacral, 4, 6, 20, 52, 86, 87
  solar plexus, 4, 8, 24, 52, 86, 87, 101, 102
  throat, 4, 10, 19, 53, 65
Children
  aura colors and, 2–3
  gold in aura of, 17
  with hyperactivity/ADHD/autism, 17
  seeing auras, 2
Claircognizance, 30
Clairvoyance, 3, 10, 55, 91
Cleansing, healing, energizing auras, 49–59
  about: overview of, 49
  cleansing aura, 57–58, 59
  crystal pendulum for, 57–59

  energizing aura, 59
  for pet auras, 94–95
Color-breathing, 68–69, 70–71, 80–81, 83, 95
Colors
  absorbing directly, 80–81
  antidote, for auras, 69–70
  for social gatherings, sources of, 78–79
Colors of auras, 1–37
  about: overview of interpreting, 1–2
  children and, 2–3
  closest to furthest from body, 104
  higher-aura colors, 12–13, 15–20
  interpreting auras and, 27–28
  seven main colors and their qualities/associations, 4–13
  subsidiary colors within aura bands, 20–25
  temporary changes in, 28–29
Colors, specific (qualities/associations, and *for pets in italics*)
  black, 24–25, *93–94*
  blue, 9–10, *90–91*
  brown, 21–22, *92–93*
  gold, 15–16
  gray, 23–24, *93*
  green, 8–9, *90*
  indigo, 10–11
  magenta, 17–18
  orange, 6, *89*
  pink, 20–21, *92*
  purple, *91–92*
  red, 5, *88–89*
  silver, 19–20
  turquoise, 18–19
  violet, 11–12
  white, 12–13
  yellow, 7–8, *89–90*
Crystals and gems
  antidote crystals, 70–71
  for aura harmony, 77–78, 79–80
  for aura health, 65, 70–71

making crystal waters, 79–80
for pet aura health, 94–95
strengthening, types and color associations, 5,
    6, (8–13), 16, (18–22), 24, 25

E

Emotional layer, 52
Energies, aura
    pure life force and, 12, 71
Energizing aura, 59
Etheric layer, 50–51
Etheric template, 53

F

Feeling auras
    psychometry and, 44–45, 54–57
Fragrances
    for aura health, 65–66, 71
    color associations, (5–7), (9–13), 16, (18–22),
        24, 25
    for happy gatherings, 78

G

Gabriel, 6, 13, 20, 62
Golden aura shields, 100–103
Grayness, creating aura of, 104–105

H

Happy gatherings, creating, 76–80
Health of auras, strengthening/maintaining,
    61–71
    about: overview of, 61
    color-breathing and, 68–69, 70–71, 80–81,
        83, 95
    colors to use and antidotes, 67–71
    crystals for, 65
    filling with light, power, harmony, 62–64
    fragrance for, 65–66
    keeping aura bright and healthy, 64–67
    for pets, 94–95
    rainbow charisma aura, 62–64
    removing pollution, 66–67
    water for, 64
Home and workplace, 73–83
    absorbing color directly, 80–81
    aura mirroring, 82–83

auras in workplace, 81–82
collective auras of, 76–77, 79, 81, 82
color sources for, 78–79
creating happy gatherings, 76–80
studying aura interactions, 73–74
tuning in to aura interactions, 74
working with auras at, 74–76

K

Ketheric template, 54

L

Layers of auras
    assessing with power of touch, 54–57
    astral layer, 53
    celestial body, 53–54
    emotional layer, 52
    etheric layer, 50–51
    etheric template, 53
    how to identify, 50–54
    illustrated, 51
    ketheric template/causal body, 54
    layers and their qualities, 50–54
    mental layer, 52
    recording findings of assessments, 56–57
Life force, pure, 12, 71

M

Mental layer, 52
Metatron, 17, 19
Michael, 13, 16, 103, 106
Mirroring, aura, 82–83
Mood aura, 27–37
    advantages of reading, 27–28
    combining personality readings and, 46–47
    identifying/seeing, 29–32
    monitoring your own, 31–32
    observing and recording findings, 32–37
    temporary color changes in, 27–28

P

Pendulum, crystal, 57–59
Personality aura, 39–47
    advantages of reading, 39, 40–41
    alterations in, 39–40
    combining mood readings and, 46–47

Personality aura, *(continued)*
  identifying aspects you most need, 40
  importance of understanding, 40–41
  ongoing aura practice, 47
  psychometry (psychic touch) for reading,
    44–45
  seeing and recording findings, 40, 42–43
  studying in detail, 41–43
  techniques to see, 42
Pets/animals, auras of, 85–95
  colors in, 88–94
  crystals to maintain health of, 94–95
  identifying layers, 85–86
  mood aura, (87–94)
  observing, 86
  personality aura, (87–94)
  sealing, 99–100
  soul aura, 88
  species aura, (87–93)
Pollution, removing from aura, 66–67
Protecting auras, 97–106
  for body, mind, spirit, 100
  creating aura of grayness, 104–105
  golden aura shields, 100–103
  of pets, 99–100
  psychic energy shield, 100–103
  rainbow ritual, 106
  sealing aura with light, 97–100
  withdrawing aura, 103–104
Psychometry
  assessing seven aura layers with, 54–57
  reading auras with, 44–45

R
Rainbow charisma aura, creating, 62–64
Rainbow ritual, 106
Raphael, 7, 62
Raziel, 23
Reading auras
  advantages of, 27–28, 39
  combining mood and personality readings,
    46–47
  observing and recording findings, 32–37
  ongoing practice, 47
Recording
  layer well-being assessments, 56–57
  mood aura findings, 32–37
  personality aura findings, 42–43

S
Sachiel, 10
Seeing auras
  children and, 2
  clairvoyance and, 2, 10
  mood aura, 29–32
  personality aura, 40, 42

W
Water, for aura health, 64
Waters, crystal, 79–80
Withdrawing aura, 103–104

Z
Zadkiel, 12